Reflecting His Image

Reflecting His Image

The Beauty of Following Christ Intimately

K. P. Yohannan

gfa books, a division of Gospel for Asia
1932 Walnut PLZ, Carrollton TX 75006 USA
phone: (972) 416-0340
fax: (972) 416-6131

Paperback:
First printing: August 1998

For current information about Gospel for Asia or gfa books,
visit our web site: www.gfa.org

B5988 988

Dedication

I would like to dedicate this book to Wolfgang Mueller, who led my wife to the Lord when she was 14 and, through his life and teaching, taught her about following Christ. Wolfgang's life has produced much fruit that remains throughout the world.

Contents

Acknowledgments

Originally much of this material was shared during Gospel for Asia's staff meetings. My wife, Gisela, compiled it into small chapters. For hours she faithfully labored. Thank you, Gisela.

Heidi Chupp helped with the editing work. Thanks, Heidi. Also thank you Tricia Bennett for the editing work that you did.

Katie McCall did the layout and cover design. I appreciate you, Katie.

And Claudia Edwards, thank you for all those hours you spent, reading over the manuscript multiple times, making sure it was ready to print.

Thank you, too, all our faithful brothers and sisters at Gospel for Asia who have stood by us all these years—without your love and labor of love, this wouldn't be possible. You are loved.

Introduction

Growing up by a river flowing with crystal-clear water, we boys swam in it almost every day. Those times added much joy to my childhood. But that was long ago, and now that river is polluted. The fish in the river are dying, and hardly anyone goes swimming there anymore.

How did this happen? Over the years the pollution that was dumped into the river caused this tragedy.

This is true of our lives also. The Lord promised that out of us rivers of living water would flow—pure and unhindered, producing and sustaining life. But unfortunately, due to both lack of watchfulness and lack of diligence on our part, the enemy has polluted our lives. Now instead of rivers of living water flowing out of us, our lives have been dragged down to mediocrity.

But if we travel up from the foot of the mountain to the source of this river, we'll find the pure crystal-clear water flowing from it. Instead of being content with superficial Christianity, we need to learn the original purpose of God for our lives. In the Word of God, we clearly read in Genesis 1:26 that the Lord made us so that we may reflect His image.

This book is a compilation of small chapters on many subjects—but they all center on the theme of following Christ closely. It is a small attempt to help those who are seeking to be real in their walk with the Lord. The last chapter is specifically written to give new hope to all who have failed, and now wonder if God will ever use them again. Nothing in this book is new except the joy I have experienced in following the truths written here. Others have gone before me and experienced the Lord in ways I long to know and learn in this pilgrimage. I follow in their footsteps.

K. P. Yohannan
Carrollton, Texas

Chapter 1

Clinging to Shadows

The earth seemed to tremble at the mighty shout of the Israelites as the priests carried the ark of the covenant into their war camp. Now the battle could begin. Their guarantee for victory had just arrived! The people cheered and celebrated. It would be just like in the days of Moses and Joshua: the ark would go before them, and no enemy, however strong he might be, had even the slightest chance of defeating the armies of Israel.

With great confidence the Israelites marched out to meet the Philistines, who were shaking in their boots, expecting to be wiped out by the God of Israel. But to everyone's amazement and horror, God was not with His people. The two priests Hophni and Phinehas, along with 30,000 soldiers, were slaughtered on the battlefield. And the enemy captured the ark of God.

What went wrong? The Israelites had counted on their past experiences and assumed that God was still with them! Their earlier shout of triumph turned out to be a vain and empty noise. Their actions seemed genuine, but in reality they were clinging to shadows from the past. All of these events were brought into focus by Phinehas' widow, who named her son Ichabod (which means *no glory*) as she was dying, saying "The glory is departed from Israel."

After this tragic defeat, the entire nation must have asked, "When did our God leave us? And why didn't we—His people—notice it sooner?"

What about us? How do we know if God is still with us like He was 10 years or two months ago?

This account from 1 Samuel 4, as well as many others, is given to us for our instruction. It is designed to clearly teach us that past experiences with God, including miracles and answers to prayer, are never proof that God is with us and sustains us today. Each and every day, our walk with the Lord and our commitment to Him must be fresh and new.

It is of utmost importance that the people who are called to fulfill God's plan and purpose remain close to Him and do not blindly rely on the past. You see, God has more than just one way of dealing with mankind. In every generation He does new things. He creates new wine, which requires new wineskins. The problem with us is that we want the new wine, but we also want to maintain the old wineskins from our past. It must be our highest priority, however, to continually maintain the freshness of our walk with Him.

Over and over we read throughout the Bible and church history how God commits Himself to an individual or a group of people. But then, somewhere along the way, His presence is no longer with them. The sign on their front door now reads "Ichabod"—the glory has departed. They may still be running all their "good," religious programs, along with preaching, shouting, and doing every kind of thing imaginable. But basically all they are doing is clinging to shadows, while He is no longer there.

It is tragic, and we feel deeply hurt, when "Ichabod," this severe judgment of God, is pronounced over a fellowship to which we belong or a Christian organization that we value. However, rather than joining them in clinging to shadows, we still have the option of moving on. But when God begins to write this word over the door of our own hearts, "Ichabod" becomes extremely personal. Once there was genuine love and reality in our worship, giving, and service to the Lord, but over time it all turned into a well-rehearsed religious performance. Others around us might not realize what has happened to us because we continue to do all the things we did before. But when God looks at our hearts, He sees an empty shell: the freshness of our walk with Him has disappeared.

What is the cause of this shift in our spiritual life? It's the same as it was for those Israelites in the Old Testament: self-centeredness. The God Who delivered them from slavery and Whom they were commanded to love supremely over all else had now become in their minds a genie to fulfill their wish for a comfortable and successful life. We fall into the same trap when we forget that we were made for Him alone. Belonging to Him means that we must lay aside all our own plans, wishes, and ambitions and out of love and with joy seek to fulfill His will instead. This keeps us coming to Him every day, asking afresh what we can do to please Him, and showing Him that He is our greatest treasure and all we desire in our lives.

Withdrawing His glory from our lives is never God's first reaction, but rather it is His last resort if we don't respond to His correction and His call to an intimate daily relationship.

But how is it possible for us to regain or to maintain this fresh walk with the Lord, if those who saw God parting the Red Sea lost it and died in the wilderness? I believe the answer starts with a conscious decision to daily "humble yourselves in the sight of the Lord" (James 4:10) and to begin or continue to "seek those things which are above, where Christ is, sitting at the right hand of God" (Colossians 3:1). And this is possible only if we are willing to repent or forsake all that caused our heart to wander away from the Lord: materialism, seeking comfort or ease, seeking others' approval and praise, spiritual pride, lack of concern for the suffering or poor, seeking honor from others, pretense . . . and all things that the Holy Spirit will remind us of as we honestly seek God. Daily seek God's approval in all areas of your life. If we practice this, restoration will take place, and His presence will remain with us.

The question is: will you act on it now, or are you going to put it off until later?

Are you clinging to shadows?

Chapter 2

God Is Not After the Majority

You can ask any pastor or evangelist what discourages him the most when he steps behind the pulpit to deliver a sermon. I believe that nine times out of 10, his answer will be "empty chairs."

Generally our success in ministry is measured by the largeness of the crowd we are able to gather, the income we can generate, the impressiveness and size of our church building, and the fame we can attach to our name.

However, when we read the Bible, we encounter a God Who longs to save the whole world but at the same time is not at all impressed by popularity and numbers. In fact, He always seems to choose to work through a minority rather than through a multitude.

One of the clearest examples of this is Gideon and his military campaign against the Midianites. The large number of volunteers who came out to join the army of Israel were not the kind of soldiers God had been looking for, and He began to send back home those who were afraid or who had knelt down to drink. We might consider these strange ways of selecting people for a battle, but God's objective was simply this: He wanted His work done only by those who wholeheartedly followed the Lord, even if the odds for victory were next to impossible. God is not at all opposed to employing thousands of His people to fight His war, but most of the time He finds the majority of them unusable.

When Jesus looked out over the huge crowd of enthusiastic followers during the Passover feast in Jerusalem, He could have been extremely satisfied with His strategy in mass evangelism and the overall success of His ministry. After all, thousands of Jews believed in His name and publicly testified to the authenticity of His miracles.

But Jesus was not at all taken by their applause, and He was not impressed by their many words of appreciation. He looked beyond their cheers for Him to the motivation of their hearts. What He discovered there caused Him to make one of the most serious decisions for the future direction of His ministry: "But Jesus did not commit Himself to them, because He knew all men" (John 2:24). He clearly discerned that the majority of His disciples followed Him only for personal blessings such as healing, free food, or even forgiveness of sin . . . whatever they could get out of Him. But these were not the qualifications He was looking for in people to entrust with the responsibility of heralding God's kingdom.

Jesus was searching for people who would love and follow Him for His sake, not their own. Out of the entire multitude, He only found 11 who had that kind of heart, and He totally committed Himself to them. He allowed them to observe and share His life, taught them privately, and revealed God's plans to them. No, they weren't ready to be apostles yet, and they were still going to make a lot of mistakes, but none of these things seemed a major problem in God's mind. You see, the greatest obstacle for God to entrust Himself to us is our hidden self-love, in even the most spiritual things as well as in our service for Him.

If we look close enough, we will discover that 99.9 percent of our Christianity today is based on what *we* can get out of it: a better family life, good kids, getting out of trouble, restored health, a wholesome lifestyle, a brighter future, security, forgiveness of sin, and finally heaven and the rewards to follow.

The question is this: where are we, and what is our heart's motivation, in the midst of this modern interpretation of discipleship? God is not after the majority of 99.9 percent, but after a minority who actually follow Christ for His sake. He will commit Himself to a few people who are totally committed to Him for the purpose of loving Him and His Son. Nothing else matters to these people. Whether they have much or little in this world, they have no other agenda.

Paul and the rest of the apostles are our examples of what God can do through a handful of people who totally belong to Him. Let us consider their singlehearted commitment to Christ and allow the Lord to shed His light on our own divided, selfish hearts. Only when we are willing to lay aside all our own "spiritual" agendas and wishes can God use us to build His kingdom.

"For the eyes of the Lord run to and fro throughout the whole earth, to show Himself strong on behalf of those whose heart is loyal to Him" (2 Chronicles 16:9).

God is still looking for a mighty minority.

Chapter 3

Authentic or Synthetic?

The plant in the clay pot looked so vibrant with such lush green color. The blooming flower was so attractive, so beautiful. I began to gravitate toward this plant. Other people in the room were engaged in conversation, but I was determined to touch the leaves and smell the flower. As I got near, the scent that came from the plant was even more inviting.

As I leaned over to touch the lush green leaves, someone from behind said, "Brother K. P., that plant is not real. It is synthetic." "No, it can't be," I said. "Then you see for yourself," he replied. Sure enough, to my shock and surprise, the plant was man-made and the fragrance artificial. It had fooled me for sure.

Today so much that passes for Christianity—Christian ministry, serving the Lord—is like this plant, that is, not authentic. It looks real and smells real, but the life of God is not in it. Man creates and sustains it by his own cleverness and strength.

Great zeal in serving God, giving money, worshiping the Lord—it all looks wonderful, yet the motivating factor is not from a deep-down inner reality.

It is all for show and to gain something for the self . . . even just a word of praise from men.

People who seem to have great zeal in serving God, giving money for a worthy cause or worshipping the Lord with devotion and joy easily impress us. Although we look with awe at the outside appearance, God searches hearts and judges motives (Jeremiah 17:10). He will reject even the best of Christian activity as a show—a means to gain glory and praise from men—if the motivating factor does not come from a pure heart. These people "draw near with their mouths and honor Me with their lips, but have removed their hearts far from Me" (Isaiah 29:13).

God is looking for those who are pure in their heart to serve and worship Him. He longs for a bride whose only goal is to please Him and be approved by Him. Her deep devotion and singleness of heart toward her soon-coming bridegroom are reflected in her overwhelming desire to do His will. Her heart's cry is, "Behold, You desire truth in the inward parts" (Psalms 51:6).

The church at Ephesus was such a bride. It had an incredible beginning. These pagans turned to the Lord with all their heart. They made a clean break and publicly burned all their false religious books and idols. Their love for Jesus didn't come cheaply. They had to pay a heavy price in following the Lord. But with joy they endured great persecution and suffering. To them, Jesus was worth the loss of all their possessions. He was more important than the whole world. God was pleased with them because their love for Him was authentic.

Yet as time went by, the Lord told them that He was going to put out their light and walk away from them. Why?

Revelation 2:1-4 tells us the answer. They were fundamental in faith, they gave freely, they were fully involved in ministry, and they worked hard. Their lives were filled with tremendous labor and activity. But it was all out of their own fleshly energy, not out of love for the Lord Himself. For this reason, Jesus rebuked them. He didn't say,

"Stop all your activity." He told them to repent of their inner carnality and shallowness and then to do the same work with a motivation that He could accept.

If all this could happen to a church that was doing so well, what about us? It is vitally important that we take a good look at ourselves and honestly examine our motivation. Is the activity we claim to do for Jesus in reality done for personal gain or honor from men? Jesus rebuked the Pharisees not for the "ministry" they did, but for the reason they did it: "How can you believe, who receive honor from one another, and do not seek the honor that comes from the only God?" (John 5:44).

Why do we so easily fall into the trap of seeking our own gain and consequently lose our pure and correct motivation? Paul explains in 2 Thessalonians 2:3-10 that it is the spirit of the antichrist, through the mystery of lawlessness, which is at work all around us, even seeking to infiltrate the church. This spirit displays Satan's foremost desire: to exalt himself over God and take His place.

Whenever we listen to the deception of this spirit, we will also seek to exalt ourselves above others and draw attention to ourselves through our excellent preaching, teaching, healing, or music ministry.

Jesus encountered the temptation of this spirit as well, but He always refused to yield. Throughout His life on earth, Jesus did everything for the glory of the Father. He did not do one thing of His own or for Himself (John 6:38). His motivation was absolutely pure. God wants us to become like Him in all things and that's why He is deeply concerned about the motivation behind our service.

So often we are careless and undiscerning when it comes to our Christian activities. We are easily fooled into thinking that if it looks good it must be real. But only a pure, authentic life can produce fruit that remains for eternity. All else will turn into ash.

You may be able to buy a bushel of apples and tie them onto a barren tree. To an onlooker, the tree will appear fruitful. Yet time will tell. Eventually, the fruit will all rot and fall to the ground. Likewise, all that is done through our carnal reasoning, human ingenuity, talents, and money may appear great and authentic in the sight of men. Yes, it may be done in the name of Jesus and for His kingdom; yet in the day of testing, this all will be turned into a pinch of ash.

"There is going to come a time of testing in Christ's Judgment Day to see what kind of material each builder has used. Everyone's work will be put through the fire so that all can see whether or not it keeps its value, and what was really accomplished" (1 Corithians 3:13, TLB). Our motives for giving, preaching, sacrificing, and doing all that we did will be exposed and examined by the Lord Himself.

Only authentic life can produce fruit that remains for eternity. Let us not forget that what is great in man's sight, God despises (Luke 16:15).

Seek only God's approval in all that we do.

Chapter 4

"Lord, Cut Me Open"

Why haven't we yet fulfilled the Great Commission? Why are we so ineffective in building God's kingdom?

Is it because we lack money or literature or because the Bible is not translated into all the world's languages? No, I don't think so.

The deepest reason is this: we who form the church—that's you and me—are not real in our walk with the Lord and in our obedience to God's Word. Unless our hearts change and we become genuine, transparent, open, and humble in our faith (and through that, in all areas of our lives), we will never make an impact on the lost world!

Many of God's people have felt a deficiency in their Christian lives, especially when they read God's expectations for them in the Bible. In order to fix this problem, they have gone from one seminar, book, conference or convention to the next, always looking for a formula or recipe to become a powerful, effective Christian overnight.

Churches have also recognized that something vital seems to be missing. In hopes of reviving their people, they constantly come up with new plans and activities. They invite the best music groups they can find, the most eloquent speakers, and even prophets to breathe new life into their congregations. But after all the excitement is over and everyday life sets in once again, nothing much has changed. So they search for new plans and new speakers, hoping for better results next time.

David had a deep longing to be close to God and to be used of the Lord. He too felt he wasn't all God intended for him to be. However, his approach to meet this spiritual need was entirely different from most of us.

David was a man who didn't go to one of the prophets—Samuel, Nathan, or Gad—to ask for a formula. He didn't invite them to hold a seminar at his palace with the hope that some of their anointing would fall on him.

David simply went into the presence of his God with a prayer that shows he knew exactly where his root problem was.

He cried, "Search me, O God, and know my heart: try me, and know my thoughts: And see if there be any wicked way in me, and lead me in the way everlasting" (Psalm 139:23-24, KJV).

David wanted to be real, not only with his outward actions, but beginning with his innermost thoughts. He recognized that his words and actions were only a reflection of his thoughts, and his thoughts were simply the evidence of what he was really like in his heart.

Therefore, David prayed and asked the Lord to try him and to cure those wrong tendencies of his heart that showed up in his thought life.

Many years later, Jesus said, "For from within, out of the heart of men, proceed evil thoughts . . ." (Mark 7:21). In other words, we reflect the true reality of who we are by what we think. Everything first happens in our thought life before it is translated into words and actions. What we speak or do is only what has been going on inside of us for a long time.

Our problem is not that we lack Bible information, speakers, or opportunities. Rather, our problem is that we don't want to face the truth of who we really are. We don't want others to know it either, and we even try to fool God. We never ask Him to search our heart and reveal our secrets. Instead, we pretend with a spiritual life we don't live, a peace we don't experience, and a holiness and commitment we don't possess.

We will never make any progress in becoming more like Jesus unless we permit God to cut us open, search our hearts, try us, know our thoughts, and then change us from the inside. Only then can we become real according to the Word of God.

That reality will make us powerful witnesses for Jesus, even if we don't say a word. We will be so transparent and so genuine that if the world around us tries us with fire, we will come out as glittering gold.

If you truly desire this reality, stop looking to plans and activities as your solution. Begin today to call out to the Lord as David did. Say, "Lord Jesus, cut me open. Please search my heart, try me, know my thoughts, reveal to me who I am, and change me, at any cost, to become what Your Word says I ought to be." Believe me, there is no prayer the Lord delights to answer for His people more than this one!

There is no anesthesia for this radical surgery.

Chapter 5

Reflecting His Image

After the initial excitement and tremendous joy over our salvation ebbs away a little, we make an amazing discovery: God isn't satisfied yet with what we look like! We learn from His Word that, "God didn't create man to tend His garden, and He didn't save us to have workers for His harvest field. God's original and sole purpose for man has always been to manifest His image."[1] That's what He is after when He begins to seriously deal with our human nature.

Perhaps at first we are confident that He can complete this job in no time at all, because we don't look so bad in our own eyes. To help us understand how far away from His likeness we really are, He shows us His true image in Scriptures like these:

> For thus says the High and Lofty One who inhabits eternity, whose name is Holy: "I dwell in the high and holy place, with him who has a contrite and humble spirit, to revive the spirit of the humble, and to revive the heart of the contrite ones" (Isaiah 57:15).

> "For all those things My hand has made, and all those things exist," says the LORD. "But on

this one will I look: on him who is poor and of a
contrite spirit, and who trembles at My word"
(Isaiah 66:2).

God actually expects His children to possess the same kind
of deep humility and total submission that Jesus had, so
that we too will have rivers of living water flow from our
lives to this dying world.

But how can we ever become like this when by our very
nature we are proud, stubborn, and selfish? In addition, we
are part of a world that has taught us from birth to fight for
our own rights; to be ambitious and unbending; and to value
success, ability, and position above all else.

The Bible tells us, without a doubt, that God is indeed
able to change us into His likeness—but only through one
way: the process of brokenness.

We must recognize that being born again is just the
beginning of God's work in us. Ninety-nine percent is yet to
be done. God is continually at work in our lives, breaking
us, changing us, and putting to death our selfish desires, until
His nature shines through.

How important really is this brokenness for our service
in God's kingdom? Could we somehow get by without it? A.
W. Tozer once said that he doubted seriously if God could
ever use a man until He had broken him thoroughly and
empowered him.

I once received a phone call from some of Gospel for Asia's
leaders in India. A very well-known, highly educated man
had showed an interest in teaching in our seminary. These
leaders wanted to know what I thought about it. I simply
said to our leadership: "As far as academics are concerned,
he would be one of the greatest assets we could have in our
school. We could not find a more intellectual man or one so
incredibly gifted and able to communicate. However, his
coming would be dangerous and disastrous for our

institution. The reason is simply this: you know as much as I do that this man is not broken. He is so self-sufficient, strong, and sure of himself. If there is an argument, he always wins. In a group, he acts important so he will be noticed.

"He has been to many places, but he's never remained anywhere. It's not because he's not able; it's due to his lack of humility. Even if he gave us thousands of dollars and begged us to allow him to teach, I would never allow it. If he were at the seminary, he would produce unbroken, stubborn students just like himself. God is not looking for able people, but for broken people."

Above all else, God's greatest concern is our brokenness. Just like our potential professor, we will only reproduce what we are ourselves. And only in the same measure in which we allow ourselves to be broken can we experience resurrection life and rivers of living waters flowing unhindered from our innermost being.

In the work of the Lord, the need to fill a position is often so great that we end up searching for someone with matching gifts and abilities but ignore their unbroken condition. What are some of the clear signs[2] of unbroken people?

• They focus on the failures of others.

• They must be in control of their situation.

• They exhibit a self-protective spirit, guarding their time, rights, and reputation. They will not allow anyone to walk into their private world.

• They are driven to be recognized and appreciated. They will do anything, even spiritually, to find that appreciation from others.

• They are wounded when others are promoted and they are overlooked. They feel confident in how much they know and feel the organization they work with is privileged to have them on staff. They are quick to blame others and defensive when criticized.

• They work hard to maintain their image and protect

their reputation. Consequently, they find it very difficult to share their real spiritual need with others. They try to make sure no one finds out about their secret sins.

• They have a hard time saying, "I was wrong; I sinned. Would you please forgive me?"

• They compare themselves with others and feel deserving of honor. They are blind to their own heart's true condition.

• They don't see any need for repentance . . . and the list goes on.

When you read this list, do you find yourself in it? By our human nature, all of us are unbroken. Our usefulness to God and our ability to reflect His likeness are directly linked to our giving Him permission to break us and our willingness to yield to God's work rather than resist it.

Take some time to open your heart before the Lord. Allow Him to shed His light on areas of your life in which you have refused His work of brokenness. Instead of fearing loss and pain, you can rejoice that God is making you more like Himself. His life can now flow through you, bringing many to His kingdom.

Rivers of living water will not flow out of us unless the earthen vessel is broken.

Chapter 6

The Foundation of All Service

I magine with me, if you will, the night before Abraham was going to sacrifice his son Isaac:

After supper Isaac rolled out his blanket and, a few minutes later, was sound asleep. Not so for Abraham, who didn't close his eyes all night. In the sky over their small camp he could see the stars shining brightly. They reminded him of the promise God had given him long ago, that one day his descendants would be just as numerous as the stars in the sky. Tears rolled down the old man's face, and he couldn't take his eyes off his beloved Isaac. He was hurting deeply. Tomorrow he would have to lay his son on an altar and plunge a knife into his heart.

How extremely difficult it would be for him to give up Isaac, but there was no complaint as he prepared to sacrifice his son to serve the Lord his God. He was willing to do it, not because he understood God's reason, but simply because the Lord had told him to. What a perfect picture of the type of intimate relationship God wants to have with us! However, this relationship is not possible without our sacrifice of true obedience to Him.

It is nearly impossible for us to picture ourselves as servants or slaves of a supreme ruler. We live in a time and culture in which we are basically the architects and masters of our own lives. Freedom of thought and speech and the right to choose our own destiny are at the very heart of our democratic constitutions. The forefathers of many nations fought and died in order to give and preserve this freedom, and we rightfully cherish it as our greatest human inheritance.

However, when it comes to our relationship with the living God, things are totally different. The Bible declares that He not only created us for Himself, but that we were bought with a price, the blood of Jesus, and therefore we are no longer our own!

We acknowledge this fact when we repent of our sins and receive the free gift of salvation. Yet even if we declare that we have submitted to Jesus as our Lord, our confessions often have hardly any impact on or relevance to our individualistic lifestyles. Basically, we still keep on doing what we want to do.

Paul's description of himself throughout his epistles as a bond servant (or freewill slave) of Jesus Christ is a totally alien concept to us. We can't even relate to his "slave thinking" whenever he expresses convictions such as this: All that I am and do in the service of my God is because He is Lord. He is my Master, and I have given up the right to run my own life.

Moreover, when we are confronted with God's call to lay down one of our own plans and follow His instead, we refuse, debate our options, or demand a logical explanation for such a costly requirement. That He alone is God, and we are not, seems to be insufficient grounds for us to submit without reservation. In fact, we frequently label the call to unconditional obedience as legalism.

No wonder our Christian walk and service are so shallow and fruitless—in spite of our Ph.D.s, our extensive personal libraries, and our participation in dozens of seminars.

What is wrong with us? Why don't we have an intimate relationship with God like Abraham, whom God called His friend? And why are we not a blessing even to our own families, when Abraham became a blessing to all nations? After all, we are God's children and His Spirit dwells in us.

I believe our root problem is that we know nothing about the fear of the Lord that Abraham had in his life. You see, Abraham never considered God as his "buddy" or as a means to get his wishes granted. Most important, Abraham never separated his personal life from his "ministry" or service to the One Who called him out of a people of idol worshipers in Ur. He willingly accepted pain, inconvenience, and sacrifice in order to worship and serve the living God.

When God told him, "Abraham, take your son, your only son, whom you love, and offer him as a sacrifice," he didn't tell anyone. He hurt deeply but accepted the pain and followed God's instructions. To obey the Lord unseen—in secret—is the foundation of genuine godly service. Abraham had a reverence for His God that did not question His purpose, lordship, or wisdom. He did not panic at the thought of how all this would affect the future. He responded with complete obedience, loving Him supremely even in the midst of his greatest pain.

Just when Abraham was about to slaughter Isaac on the altar, God held him back and said to him, "Now I know that you fear God" (Genesis 22:12). The literal translation of this verse actually says, "Now I know that you are a fearer of God." God definitely knew beforehand that Abraham would be willing to follow through with this ultimate sacrifice, but Abraham himself needed to know for sure how far his commitment to God would go. And it is extremely important for us to hear, from God's mouth, the bottom line of Abraham's obedience: the fear of God.

For each of us to build our life, family, future, and service on the correct foundation, we too must understand what it means to walk in the fear of the Lord.

Luke 2:40 says this about Jesus: "And the Child grew and became strong in spirit, filled with wisdom; and the grace of

God was upon Him." How did this happen? Psalm 111:10 tells us, "The fear of the LORD is the beginning of wisdom," and Hebrews 5:7 testifies that Jesus had this godly fear during His life on earth.

Furthermore, when Paul talks about authentic ministry in 2 Corinthians 7:1 he writes, "Let us cleanse ourselves from all filthiness of the flesh and spirit, perfecting holiness in the fear of God." We cannot become like Abraham or Jesus without submitting to the fear of the Lord in this manner!

But how can we even begin to develop this fear of God, which compels us to obey God just because He is Lord?

When God first called Abraham, he had the fear of idol and demon gods in him, but not yet the fear of the true and living God. After all, he didn't know Him or His nature of righteousness and love. Considering this, God did not tell Abraham at their first encounter that down the road He was going to ask Abraham to sacrifice his son. You see, Abraham first had to grow in his closeness with God and come to a place in which they were very intimate friends before God could entrust to him such a request.

A definite start in our quest for the fear of the Lord is walking with Him one step at a time and practicing obedience with a joyful heart and without complaints. Our thinking about our rights must drastically change as well. Actually, we need nothing short of a revelation in our spirit of what it means to be bought with a price—and I believe God will give that to us if we ask Him! Truly recognizing our place and God's position will place in our hearts the reverence and fear of God that we so desperately need to walk in obedience as Abraham did.

Our true service, that which lasts throughout eternity and brings multitudes to Jesus, originates from an Abraham-like sacrifice: a willingness to offer all we are and all we have for His purpose. This sacrifice starts with the fear of God in our hearts.

It is time for us to recognize that the God we serve is also a consuming fire.

Chapter 7

How Narrow Is the Narrow Road?

Have you ever wondered how narrow the narrow road is that Jesus talks about in Matthew 7:13-14?

Most of us have discovered that indeed the gate is small that leads to life. We've tried our best either with works of self-righteousness or with man-made philosophies to prove otherwise. But we finally came to the conclusion: "Nor is there salvation in any other, for there is no other name under heaven given among men by which we must be saved" (Acts 4:12). We called on the name of Jesus, entered through the narrow gate, and received salvation and eternal life.

However, as soon as we walked through the gate, we made the discovery that the road behind that gate was even more narrow than we thought. We started to walk on it thinking it might broaden as we got farther along, but it didn't.

We looked around to see how other Christians were handling this precarious path. To our astonishment, we found out that most people who call themselves Christians had construction crews deployed on both sides of the narrow road working very hard to enlarge and widen it.

When we asked them why they were doing this, they

said, "We are dealing with a modern world that has different needs and expectations than in the past. We are called to minister to people when they come to Christ, and we must do all we can to make them feel comfortable and welcome. After all, we are competing with a world out there that has everything to offer. If we tell them about picking up the cross and denying themselves or giving up everything and laying down their lives for the sake of Christ and the Gospel, we will definitely lose them. These old views of Christianity were a misunderstanding of Scripture and don't fit any longer. As Christians we deserve the best of everything in this life as well as in the next life."

Believing this lie, we have tried to make the narrow road wider and wider to accommodate all our wants, dreams, and wishes.

To many, God has become a servant to fulfill all of our expectations. Our church buildings cost millions of dollars, our Christian programs, entertainment, and resources are the best in the world, and we are very proud of these achievements. Our personal and family lives are structured to meet our desires of comfort and ease. For far too many, the narrow road has slowly become so wide that it is hard to distinguish it from the broad one!

What does all this mean for the unreached peoples of our generation who have never heard the Gospel of Jesus Christ?

It means no one cares for them, no one sacrifices on their behalf, and no one will tell them the wonderful news of God's love and salvation. Have we become so self-centered and so insensitive that we can no longer hear the call of Jesus to give up our lives for those who have never heard His name?

Even if we still can hear His call, we naturally reject and walk away from anything that requires pain and suffering or that threatens our comfort.

Oh yes, we may put a $10 bill in the offering plate when a

missionary speaks at our church, and we may donate a sweater for the homeless. But is that the extent of our compassion and personal involvement? If so, our heart is far, far away from the love of God, who willingly went to the cross to give His blood for our redemption.

We must remember that God Himself never enlarged His small gate or His narrow road. They remain the same as they were 2,000 years ago when Jesus first described them. In Matthew 7:14, He said that only a few will ever find this road.

That is so true. But there are even fewer who are willing to consider walking on the narrow road after they have found it. Deciding to choose the narrow path means they will have to walk alone while others enjoy traveling comfortably on their enlarged versions. Today, in a world with mega churches and multiplied millions of Christians, only a few will ever stop to hear the call of Christ to lay down their lives for a lost world. He might ask us to go, to support missionaries, to intercede in prayer, or to invest our strength as well as our means in order to win the lost. Recognizing that it will cost us a high price, we go to our church and to other believers for counsel.

There are wonderful pastors and elders who will encourage us to go and pursue God's call. But more often than not, we are counseled to do the opposite. We are told that if we go, no one will be able to replace us in the fellowship; and if we give our resources, the church's programs will suffer. If we get involved in pursuing missions, we won't be able to do justice to our church duties.

Maybe you've heard this call of Jesus on your life, but you were truly concerned over who would take your place if you "sold out completely." Believe me, there are others who are just as qualified as you who can take your place. But there are so very, very few who know or understand what you know. George Verwer, the founder of Operation Mobilization, once said, "It might be hard to find one in 10,000 or a million who will understand that half of the world has never heard the name Jesus and are plunging into eternal hell, and who will give their lives away to die and be unknown, unnoticed for their sake."

This statement is so true. Only a few will ever hear the call and choose the narrow road that leads to life, not only for themselves but for the lost world as well.

You plus God make a majority. Choose the narrow path—the Son of God left His footprints on it. At the end of the road, you will meet Him.

What are the things that are holding you back?

Chapter 8

Keeping the War in Mind

Can you imagine an airline pilot flying a 747 over the Atlantic Ocean and in the middle of the flight forgetting his destination?

One of the strongest and most successful attacks of the enemy on the work of God is to cause us to forget our purpose and our goal. All of a sudden we find ourselves totally wrapped up in "normal living," no longer able to answer the question "Why are we here? What are we doing?"

The Bible very clearly tells us that we are here not for ourselves but for the cause of a lost world that has never heard the name of Jesus and for its multiplied millions of souls who are heading for hell.

How can we forget nations like Myanmar, Bangladesh, Nepal, Tibet, Bhutan, and China, where there is so much spiritual darkness and physical suffering? How can we so comfortably live for ourselves while millions slip into an eternal hell? We can do it because our enemy has managed to replace our purpose as a Christian with a desire for comfort and self-realization.

You see, the main motivation for us to do something is the emergency, the crisis for example, seeing the burning house where our own child is trapped inside.

Once we forget how real hell is and what it would mean

to take millions with us to heaven instead of letting them
die without Jesus, we become self-centered. From that
moment on, everything God asks us to do that would disturb
our "heaven on earth" becomes a burden, a problem to us.
We start looking for excuses to say "no, not me."

During World War II, the people of England saw that if
they didn't win the war, they would lose their land, their
freedom, and everything that was dear to them. This
realization caused them as a nation to scale down their
lifestyles to the barest of essentials. For this one goal—to
save their nation—they gladly sacrificed all they had: money,
gold, silver, even their sons to fight the war.

This type of single-focused sacrifice is often manifested
on the mission field. Shankar was born in a leper colony to
parents stricken with leprosy. In order to save him from
contracting the disease, a native missionary raised him in a
home he had built for the children of lepers. Shankar received
a good education and with it a chance to make a better life
for himself.

Along the way Shankar gave his life to the Lord and
received a call to full-time ministry. Just before his graduation
from Bible school, the missionary brother told him that he
was free to go to a new place and start a new Gospel work.
Shankar replied, "No, I will work among my own people,
the lepers, and tell them how the Lord has changed my life
and how He can save them." Today Shankar has laid down
everything he has gained and his chance for a better life to
live and work as a missionary in the leper colonies of India.

He remembered the war.

We too must keep the war in our mind—at all times. Let
us not forget why we are here. God is looking for people
with a wartime commitment which will save our generation.

What about you? Are you willing to stand in the gap for a
person, a village, a state or a nation? The Lord was looking for
a person who was willing to make such a commitment when

He spoke through the prophet Ezekiel and said, "So I sought for a man among them who would make a wall, and stand in the gap before Me on behalf of the land, that I should not destroy it; but I found no one" (Ezekiel 22:30).

Make a list of 10 people who don't know the Lord and pray for them daily—fast and pray. Witness to people about the Lord wherever you are. Carry Gospel tracts or booklets and pass them out. Find out about the unreached nations and people groups of the world and adopt them as your prayer focus. Pray and believe for their salvation.

You are called. What are you waiting for?

Chapter 9

Starting from Zero

Each one of us would be absolutely terrified if we were asked to walk along the edge of the Grand Canyon during a pitch-dark night without any light. After all, we could fall off the cliff and die. We might be more willing to do it if we had a travel plan and a bright light that would allow us to see every detail ahead of us.

In the same way, we want to plan and control our lives while we walk with the Lord. We want to be sure of tomorrow, and we want to be certain how He is going to take care of us before we ever dare to step out on His Word. We don't mind that He is our King as long as His actions are predictable and He shows and explains to us His schedule ahead of time.

On the other hand, we feel helpless, frustrated, and almost angry if all we hear from Him is "follow Me, trust Me" and "walk by faith, not by sight." We have waited for details, plans, and especially security, but all He gave us was His promise that He is all we need.

True walking with the Lord requires us to be totally stripped of everything that is of ourselves and in which we had put our trust, as well as our expectations of acceptance, approval, security, importance, abilities, and our rights.

Being stripped does not at all mean to renounce the world and go somewhere to live in a cave. It simply means that we look at ourselves and recognize that we have nothing in us to stand on and nothing to hold on to. All we have is total emptiness. Once we recognize this truth, we are then in the right position to follow Him, totally depend on Him, and trust completely in His sufficiency.

God deliberately waited until Abraham was 100 years old and Sarah 90 before He gave them a son. He waited until there was no doubt that Abraham was aware of his own emptiness and therefore was totally dependent on God. Isaac became the son of the Spirit and not of the flesh.

Throughout the Bible we find examples of how God had to wait until His people came to the place of recognizing their own emptiness before He was able to lead them, give them victory, and show Himself mighty on their behalf. At times God had to intervene to speed up this process, such as in the story of Gideon. God reduced Gideon's army to 300 men to make it impossible for them to win the battle in their own strength.

How about you? Have you stepped on empty ground?

1. Is there something the Lord has asked you to do but you put it off because you feel either unqualified or that you will lose control of the situation?

2. What has hindered you from giving unselfishly to reach the lost in our generation?

3. Can you honestly say, "This world is not my home. I am just passing through"?

4. If someone were to point a gun at you and say, "Deny Christ or I will kill you," what would be your response? Can you say as Paul did, ". . . Nor do I count my life dear to myself" (Acts 20:24)?

5. Is your prayer life proof of your total dependence on the Lord? Do you ask the Lord to show you His plans with a willing heart to obey them, or do you just ask Him to bless your plans?

God has never accepted the product of the flesh, and He

never will, however good it might look in our sight. Our plans, our strength, and our works, based on anything we find in ourselves, will all burn up. Only that which is of the Spirit will remain eternally.

If we want to follow Him, we must stand on empty ground. It is only in this way that all the results will be of the Spirit and all glory will be the Lord's, not our own.

> The Lord says: Cursed is the man who puts his trust in mortal man and turns his heart away from God. He is like a stunted shrub in the desert, with no hope for the future; he lives on the salt-encrusted plains in the barren wilderness; good times pass him by forever. But blessed is the man who trusts in the Lord and has made the Lord his hope and confidence. He is like a tree planted along a riverbank, with its roots reaching deep into the water—a tree not bothered by the heat nor worried by long months of drought. Its leaves stay green and it goes right on producing all its luscious fruit (Jeremiah 17:5-8, TLB).

A warning such as this we must not ignore.

Chapter 10

Giving Up the Good

"This is the beginning of the end." You have read it many times, you probably have heard many preachers say it. And possibly you have even said it yourself. The question is, the end of what? As is often the case, we use words and phrases without really thinking about what they mean.

"The end" does not mean the completion of a journey, or the end of some war that is raging, or the finish of any other thing that happens as a part of life's events. In this phrase, "the end" refers to the disappearance of time as we know it. Soon the prophecy in the book of Revelation will come to pass, ". . . and time shall be no more."

I'm shaken with this thought, knowing that there are billions of people living in my generation who do not know the Lord Jesus Christ. They are rushing toward eternity, helplessly chained inside a house that is on fire. If they are not rescued, the end result for them will be eternal weeping, wailing, and pain. Yet there need not be. Jesus died for them. I'm told to rescue them. I am supposed to walk into the fire and pull them out. Seconds tick by, and soon it will be too late. I hear their agony and their cries for help.

Now we have begun this new year of 1998. Last year incredible events were happening around the world that signaled "the beginning of the end." There is no time to sit, to think, or to plan—but only to move as fast as we can to win the lost. Time is running out. I believe the Lord is calling His people to commit their lives with absolute, all-out dedication to reach the lost and dying of our generation. However, as C. S. Lewis said, "Active habits are strengthened by repetition but passive ones are weakened. The more often (a man) feels without acting, the less he will be able ever to act, and, in the long run, the less he will be able to feel."[1]

In North America, we are inundated with Christian books, conferences, and programs that keep us continually occupied. Eventually we become overly familiar with the things of God.

It was the same in Jesus' time. So many voices called for His attention. He received so much advice and was enticed with so many good things, but He rejected it, and said, "For the Son of Man has come to seek and to save that which was lost" (Luke 19:10). And we read in Romans 8:29, "For whom He foreknew, He also predestined to be conformed to the image of His Son, that He might be the firstborn among many brethren." That is, you and I must become like Jesus. And as we become like Jesus, we will say "no" to many good things and commit our lives with an undivided heart and determination to reach multiplied millions who are dying and going to hell having never heard of Jesus' death for them.

What are the many good things that are keeping you from the best and the most important?

May I challenge you, as I have challenged my own staff at Gospel for Asia, to recommit your life without any reservation to reach our generation for the Lord Jesus Christ? There is a price to pay. There is pain. There is agony. Tears. Hurts. Disappointments. Loss. But it's all worth it. This battle is intense; it is hard. But it will not last very long. Time is running out.

Decide to pray daily for different countries of the world. Request the SEND!™ newsmagazine we send out bi-monthly to help you pray with us. Live more simply. Don't be caught up in and enticed by the world's advertising. Ask the question, "Why do I need it?" Give more this year to support missionaries who are giving their lives to reach the world's lost souls.

Please walk away from the lukewarm, selfish, "me, mine, and ours" Christianity and dedicate yourself to a radical, all-out commitment to walk in His footsteps. His footsteps will take you to genuine, intense warfare that will cost you much, but in the end this is the best thing you can do. As Dietrich Bonhoeffer said, "When Christ calls a man, he bids him come and die."[2]

Consider the commitment of the Nepali brothers:

> As a chilly wind started to blow over the steep mountain trail, the two men hurried to reach an area that was sheltered by huge rocks in which to bed down for the night. Just as the last glimpses of daylight disappeared, they reached their destination and gladly set their heavy back loads on the ground.
>
> Extremely tired from the all-day climb, they hastily ate dinner, wrapped themselves in blankets, and went to sleep. At sunrise they had already resumed their difficult and often dangerous trek, ascending higher and higher into the mountainous Mustang region of northern Nepal.
>
> Aaitaman and Suk Bahadur are porters carrying supplies from Pokhara, the last bus station on the way to the Loba tribal village of Jomsom, a six-day climb on foot.
>
> But there is much more to their lives than carrying loads on their back and earning a living the hard way. These two young men are the answers to your prayers for God to send

missionaries to the Loba tribal people!

After receiving a clear call from the Lord to work among this unreached people group, these two native missionaries from the Gorkha district traveled by bus to Pokhara and then walked for six days to the mountain village of Jomsom. Their plan was to settle there and pioneer a church. But things were not as easy as they thought.

They quickly found out that the local people would not allow outsiders to stay among them unless they had a job in the village. The brothers searched for employment, but nothing was available except carrying supplies like rice, salt, and other provisions from the base of the mountain to the village at the top. For the sake of the Gospel and their love for the Loba people, Aaitaman and Suk Bahadur, graduates from the Gospel for Asia Nepali Bible school, accepted the job.

Every month they walk 15 days up and down the mountain, carrying heavy loads on their back—and witnessing about Jesus to every one they meet on the way. So far they have covered five Loba villages with the Gospel.

Their labor for Jesus has not been in vain; with the first few people they won to Christ, they were able to start a small fellowship in Jomsom.[3]

Jesus asks no less commitment from us, for He gave His all, including His life, to save the lost.

Chapter 11

Commitment Plus Sacrifice Equals Victory

As she was overpowered by the soldiers of the Sri Lankan army, the woman struggled desperately to swallow a deadly cyanide pill from her necklace, but to no avail.

She was a well-known Tamil Tiger, a guerilla fighter. She lived for a single cause: the war to gain homeland rule for the Tamil population of Sri Lanka. After her capture, an official of the Sri Lankan government visited her in prison. As he talked to her, he was amazed by her absolute commitment to the cause. She didn't beg him for her life, and she did not offer valuable secret information to save her skin. Fully aware of her impending execution, she appealed to him: "Please help our cause. When we are in power, we will remember you."

He asked her why she had joined the liberation movement, she gave him the following explanation: "I was in my late 20s, well-educated and working as a medical doctor. Then one day my whole life was changed when my parents were killed by soldiers. I left my profession and everything I knew, and I subjected myself to vigorous training to become a freedom fighter."

It was from the very official who had met this woman in prison, that I learned about this encounter. This story challenged me afresh to think very deeply about the meaning of commitment to a cause and the willingness to sacrifice all in the attempt to accomplish it.

Of course, this guerilla fighter was giving her life for an earthly, ideological goal. Her dreams might never come to pass. Even if they would materialize, they would all be for the here and now. None of those dreams would last for eternity.

Jesus has not asked us to follow Him for a cause whose outcome is uncertain or questionable. Instead, He has already won the victory over Satan, sin, and death through the cross and His resurrection. With His life, He portrayed the elements needed to win any kind of spiritual victory: total commitment to God and His purpose, and unrestricted willingness to sacrifice everything to accomplish victory.

Jesus not only lived this truth, but over and over, He also taught it to His disciples and anyone who considered following Him. He wanted to make sure that we clearly understand that there is no other key to spiritual victory and no other way to fulfill our responsibility to proclaim His kingdom here on earth. To choose Him above all else and to love Him more than our own lives—this is the commitment required to be able to do His will. The sacrifice needed to accomplish His cause is none other than what Jesus told us in John 12:24: "Unless a grain of wheat falls into the ground and dies, it remains alone; but if it dies, it produces much grain."

When we read the New Testament, we cannot overlook the most direct application of this teaching in the lives of the apostles and the early Christians. As they took the Gospel into all the world, it caused them to regard suffering, agony, and even martyrdom as privileges. They knew that tremendous victory and fruit would be produced for eternity as a result.

Think what Christ could accomplish through your church—and in your own life—if you would accept such commitment and sacrifice as the means to victory! What would happen if a church would joyfully decide to be satisfied with a modest building, wooden benches, and the barest of essentials instead of spending millions on a palace of comfort and prestige? What if that church were to use the money saved to help reach those who had never heard the Gospel before? And what if that church's members did all this out of love for Christ? I believe they would discover that their sacrifice brought them greater joy sitting on wooden benches than they could have ever experienced on the most costly pews.

What would happen if you would first run your plans and wishes for a comfortable, secure life through the filter of commitment and sacrifice? Think about the time and money you want to spend on entertainment, trips, cars, home decorating, and clothes. Could it be that you would discover greater joy and satisfaction without these things, if you chose instead to pray and fast for a lost world or to spend your resources to help win souls in the most unreached areas?

We actually deceive ourselves when we think that our clever strategies, conferences, and token offerings of time and money will win this world for Christ.

There is no substitute for sacrifice if we care to follow the Son of God, who set His face to the cross and its shame.

Taking up the cross is the ultimate form of self-denial.

Chapter 12

Motivations

Almost daily we are exposed by television, radio, or newspapers to disasters, famines, and much human suffering around the world. And added to this, we are reminded frequently of the millions who die daily without ever hearing the Gospel of Christ.

But as followers of Christ, we know that we can't just "walk away and forget it." Therefore, many of us get personally involved or give to various causes, ministries, and organizations.

But as a Christian, have you ever examined yourself and honestly answered the question, "Why do I give, pray, or get involved in this or that activity for the kingdom of God?" Is it because the cause presented is so urgent or desperate? Is it because of some internal guilt feeling? Or is it because you are so overpowered by compassion or pity?

All these reactions are normal human responses; but, according to the Bible, they are not good enough reasons to give to the Lord!

Then, of course, there is one more reason that probably motivates more believers to do good works than any of the above. This "reason" is that we are told that God is in terrible trouble and we need to help Him out! The appeal usually goes something like this:

"Things" are going to crumble . . . Christian media programs will have to go off the air . . . building projects will be shut down . . . social programs can no longer be continued . . . souls will go to hell, if you don't give now.

This is actually an appeal to our unbelief. And worst of all, we are reminded that if these things happen, God's glory will be gone, and the devil will win—unless, of course, we come to the rescue!

Now, I don't doubt that a number of those projects would not be able to continue without these kinds of appeals! Sadly, we have been trained for decades to give to this kind of request—and too many Christians only give when they hear needs presented in this faithless way. But I also believe the main reason some of those projects would "go under" is because God never ordained them in the first place! Or maybe He is trying to get our attention because He wants to create something newer or better.

I've always believed that God is not in any financial trouble. We never need to panic, thinking that somehow we need to help Him out of a tight spot. He has made no promise that He is not able to keep. God is not helplessly looking at a lost world hoping that someone will finally feel guilty enough to do something. He promised that His kingdom will never fall— and the gates of hell will not prevail against His church. He has enough power to complete whatever He sets out to do.

God is not the One in trouble—we are. We don't understand that He doesn't want our money unless He can have our hearts first!

Isaiah would be shocked. Ezekiel would be shaken. Jeremiah would be shattered. If these prophets were alive today, they would barely believe what their eyes would see. There is an abomination in the household of God.

Unsaved marketing experts write appeal letters for money-starved ministries . . .

Huge computer printers spew out mass produced "personal prophetic words" by the thousands . . .

Women in skin tight bodysuits advertise the latest in "Christian aerobics" . . .

TV preachers in costly apparel promise you riches if you send tithes to their ministry . . .

The blood-washed Church of the Son of God has gone Madison Avenue. Let the prophets weep and wail! The mighty have fallen—and fallen and fallen. Who would have thought we could have stooped so low?

The children of the Lord are hiring out the people of the world to help raise funds for the work of God. Sons of darkness are being consulted on how to merchandise the gospel of light. The hand of God has become attached to an arm of flesh. How can this possibly be?

There was a talented young man in the fund raising industry. He had written many outstanding appeals for religious and secular clients alike. His prize winning letters hung framed on his office wall. He knew how to bring in the bucks. But he didn't know the Lord at all.

He had just finished writing an emergency plea for a prominent international ministry when he received word that his Christian grandmother was dying. He rushed to her side. But she had only one concern. She had to get her social security check mailed out to that very ministry before she died. She had just received their urgent appeal. They desperately needed her help. Could her grandson please send out the funds—before it was too late?

Little did she know that it was not her beloved "TV pastor" who wrote the letter. Little did she know that she was being moved by worldly psychological pressure and not the Spirit. And that young man, her own grandson, was to blame.

He was so shaken up when he saw the effects of his letter that he said, "Never again." He swore off the business for life. But the ministry that hired him just marched right on. How many other dying grandmothers did they plunder? How many poor widows sent in their last dollar? And how much of that money was paid out to the marketing company? How much actually went into the work of the Lord?[1]

God could easily do all His work by Himself without our involvement. After all, He spoke the world into existence. He doesn't need us to get Him out of a disaster. Some of us have our theology all wrong. We don't understand the role that God has created for us—submission to Him and utter dependence on Him in all we do and undertake.

God has commanded the church to evangelize the lost because He wants to give us the privilege of learning to obey Him and to love this needy world as He does. He wants His people to participate with Him in the redemption of the world!

It is our greatest privilege, then, to serve Him out of love.

Because we have failed to understand this great truth, we serve Him with the wrong motives. No wonder so much of the church today lacks commitment. No wonder our own personal Christian walks lack power and joy. With wrong motives, our service for Christ naturally has become a burden—and even a guilt trip for many.

Let us once again return to loving the Lord above all our programs, possessions, and our very lives. Then our service, our giving, and our praying will turn from being a burden into the greatest privilege and joy we have on this earth.

Remember, you are not your own.

"Some trust in chariots, and some in horses; but we will remember the name of the Lord our God" (Psalm 20:7).

Let God be God in your life.

Chapter 13

Anyone Can Criticize

Sixty thousand football fans fill the stadium to watch the most exciting event of the year—the Super Bowl. While spectators relax in their seats, drink their favorite soft drinks, and eat their popcorn, the two teams in front of them are involved in the hardest battle of their lives. Each player is giving his utmost. Each tries his best to catch the football, run almost world-record speeds to score points, and risk everything he has to win the game and a Super Bowl ring. The players are desperate in their efforts, regarding hard work, sweat, agony, physical exhaustion, and possibly even injury as part of their pursuit of glory.

While these 22 men race across the field, covered with dirt, giving their all, the 60,000 spectators contribute absolutely nothing to the game, except some cheers . . . and their expert criticism. Very few of them would have even a fraction of the athletic ability to take the place of one of those players, but they consider themselves qualified to criticize every move these 22 men make. The truth is, any fool can criticize, but it takes someone with character, discipline, and willingness to work hard and truly accomplish something.

In our world, it seems impossible to escape criticism. If we do poorly at school or at work, people will criticize us.

Should we do well and excel in business, we still face criticism from people who are jealous of our success. It seems to be a favorite pastime of the human race to take one person after another, good or bad, and "skin them alive" with criticism.

What makes people act this way? Psychologists say one of the underlying reasons people criticize each other is to take revenge for the hurts they once received. Whether deserved or not, criticism is always painful. No one likes it. Yet people seem to enjoy themselves when others are cut down.

Most believers have accepted the fact that the world will criticize us regardless of how saintly we may live or how many charitable contributions we may make. However, I have found that the greatest shock and discouragement for believers come when they realize that they encounter this same heartless criticism from their brothers and sisters in the Body of Christ. Of course, God never meant this to happen. But many Christians have never allowed the Lord to cleanse their lives from this destructive behavior. It's a very serious problem; and if it is not dealt with, it easily can destroy a church.

Imagine this: Jesus, the sinless Son of God, faced His worst criticism—not from the Roman government or from ungodly people—but from the most recognized and pious religious leaders of His nation. Paul experienced the same thing. His worst critics were people inside the church, not the heathen he tried to win. In fact, he deals very thoroughly with this problem in his second letter to the church in Corinth.

Perhaps you have served the Lord with all your heart in your local church or in a mission organization. You have truly poured out your life in service to others. While you were doing your very best, others around you behaved like those spectators at the football game. They watched you fight the battle; and instead of encouraging your efforts, they criticized everything you tried to do.

Whether criticism comes from the world or from within

the church, it is important for us to know how we should respond to it. The Bible clearly instructs us in Romans 12:17 not to pay back evil for evil, which means we must not lash out and respond in anger in the same manner we were treated. On the contrary, God wants us to respond differently. We are to maintain our love for the brothers and trust the Lord to handle our defense. Only if we do this will the cycle of destructive criticism be broken.

The feelings of deep hurt and discouragement that follow criticism can easily bring us to a point of despair, giving up our calling, or even suicide. In no way must we allow this to happen! If we give in, the enemy has reached his goal of stopping us from building God's kingdom.

Let us take Jesus and the apostle Paul as our examples and act like they did when they were confronted with severe criticism. They never allowed these things to hinder or stop them from following God's call. Their allegiance and faithfulness were to God alone, and independent from whatever others said. With their total focus fixed on the goal set before them, they were able to endure until the end and fulfill their calling.

Paul shared openly in his letter to the church in Corinth about the criticism he faced from some of that church's self-appointed leaders. In 2 Corinthians 10:7-18, he addressed the issue of being belittled by them and having his authority questioned. If we read his response to their accusations, we cannot help but recognize that Paul wasn't threatened by their criticism. He knew exactly who he was in Christ, what position he held in God's kingdom, and how much authority he had received from the Lord as an apostle. He didn't try to impress his critics or the church by fighting for his rights or proving his superiority. He felt totally secure in his position and would have simply told them: "Whether I am absent or present with you, I am the same Paul. There is no pretense or games with me. I live what I am in Christ, and that's all."

The best we can do when we receive criticism is to look at it objectively. If the accusations are simply empty talk, we should dismiss them and by God's grace go on with our life. On the other hand, if there is any truth in the criticism, let us be willing to change, improve, and grow in that area.

As believers, we are commanded to love and serve one another, just as Jesus did. That doesn't mean we're supposed to close our eyes when we see a brother or sister err. The Lord has given us the responsibility to watch out for each other so that all of us will win the race. This includes helping one another to correct mistakes and overcome defeats. However, to accomplish this, we are allowed to use only constructive criticism and never any words that will destroy our brother or sister. Constructive criticism flows out of a deep love and genuine concern for the person who needs help. It's never associated with gossip, revenge, or anger.

Jesus used this kind of criticism with His disciples when they slept instead of prayed or totally lacked faith for a situation. However, He talked to them in private, with gentleness and a readiness to forgive, bear their shortcomings, and even wash their feet. He had their best interests in mind and was willing to lay down His life for each of them. His goal was to build them up in every way possible. Even when He had to correct them often and they felt terrible after they failed, they always knew He did it out of love so they could grow.

We must truly have the mind of Christ when we deal with other believers and the world around us. Anyone can criticize, but we have received the power of God to build up. Let's use it!

Remember the words of Christ in John 8:7: "He who is without sin among you, let him throw a stone at her first."

Chapter 14

God Didn't Do It!

Lok Bahadur, a man from the country of Nepal, had been suffering from severe back pain for three years. As he began listening to Gospel for Asia's daily Nepali radio program, he learned that Jesus was the Son of God. That's when Lok decided to join the broadcaster in a prayer to Jesus. He simply asked the Lord to heal his back.

A few weeks later our Nepali office received a letter from Lok. With great joy he reported that Jesus had heard his prayer and healed him completely!

For us it's always an encouragement and a challenge to witness how God delights in answering the prayers of people who often know so little about Him. He responds to their simple faith in Him and the Word of God they have heard.

Whenever Jesus taught His disciples about prayer and serving God, He listed two specific groups of people they were not to imitate. The first group was the Pharisees, whom He often labeled as hypocrites. The second group was the Gentiles living across the border.

I have no doubt that the disciples immediately understood why the Gentiles were totally off course with their idol worship, long and repetitive prayers, and unholy lifestyle. But when Jesus marked the Pharisees as bad examples, He must have shocked everyone who heard Him.

After all, the Pharisees knew the Scriptures like no one else. In fact, they devoted their whole lives to studying the law. They faithfully prayed, fasted, gave alms, and tried to keep every requirement they could find. For Peter and the rest of the disciples, it was inconceivable that God could require an even higher level of commitment and service from them. No one could do more!

But Jesus was not looking for a greater number of good works from His followers. Rather, He desired their lives and service to be more effective than that of the Pharisees.

First, He wanted them to be real and to serve God out of love and with all of their hearts. Second, He wanted them to do everything by faith.

That's where the Pharisees had their blind spot and were dead wrong. They believed God accepted them on the basis of their own righteousness, generated by their effort to keep the law. They never understood Genesis 15:6, "And he [Abraham] believed in the LORD; and He accounted it to him for righteousness." Hebrews 11:6 makes it even more plain: "But without faith it is impossible to please Him [God]."

For us who have received salvation through faith in Jesus, to continue walking by faith should be easy. But that's where we miss it the most. Whenever we fail to enter the realm of faith in our prayer life and service to God, everything we do or accomplish remains in the realm of the physical: our own selves.

Perhaps we don't realize the seriousness of our "great works" done without faith. Hebrews 4:2 explains that even chaos, destruction and death can result if we do not combine God's Word and faith in our hearts: "For indeed the gospel was preached to us as well as to them; but the word which they heard did not profit them, not being mixed with faith in those who heard it."

Consider the Israelites. Can you imagine several million people who left Egypt, crossed the Red Sea, were fed by manna from heaven, and were led by a pillar of fire at night and a pillar of cloud by day? They encountered God, made a covenant with Him, received the law, and defeated every enemy with His help.

After a short trip, they arrived excitedly at the border of their promised land. Just a few more days and they would enter in. All they were waiting for was the report of the 12 spies Moses had sent ahead of them. With great anticipation they welcomed the men back and gathered to hear what they had found out on their mission.

"There are giants in the land and huge, fortified cities," 10 of them reported. "It's impossible for us to defeat them." Those few words started a riot. The other two men, Joshua and Caleb, tried their best to persuade the people to put their faith in God and believe His promises. But it was too late—the damage was already done. The people's hearts were defiled by the negative reports.

The rest of the story and the account of what happened to the Israelites, are written in Numbers 14. First, they never entered their promised land. Second, God gave them exactly what they had asked for when they had grumbled, "Would God that we had died . . . in this wilderness!" (Numbers 14:2, KJV). They had to wander 40 years in the desert until that entire generation had died, except for Joshua and Caleb.

We might ask ourselves, "Why did God do such a cruel thing to these people? What possible enjoyment could He get out of it?"

God didn't do it! They themselves caused it to happen! You see, the living God is bound and restricted by His own Word. That's the reason He has said, "But the just shall live by his faith" (Habakkuk 2:4).

The commentary on this law is the account in Hebrews 4:2: "But the word which they heard did not profit them, not being mixed with faith in those who heard it." They died without another chance.

This verse is probably the most serious warning for us as believers. You see, we too have received God's promises for our lives and our service for Him:

• If our family is unsaved: "Believe on the Lord Jesus Christ, and you will be saved, you and your household" (Acts 16:31).

• If we are in need of healing: "And by His stripes we are healed" (Isaiah 53:5).

• When we have needs: "And my God shall supply all your need . . . " (Philippians 4:19).

• When we feel lonely: "I am with you always, even to the end of the age" (Matthew 28:20).

• If we lack strength: "But those who wait on the LORD shall renew their strength" (Isaiah 40:31).

• For our ministry: "Every place that the sole of your foot will tread upon I have given you" (Joshua 1:3).

The Bible contains hundreds of promises that God is eager to fulfill in our lives as we walk with Him. Yet we will never see a single one come to pass unless the Word we have received from Him is united by faith in our hearts.

Only those who are weak in themselves can believe God for the impossible.

Chapter 15

When Can We Retire?

"When can we retire?" This is a very real question for us, because we are living in a society in which we have been taught to plan carefully toward a time in our lives when we will have less stress, less responsibility, less work, and more time for ourselves.

What about a retirement plan from fighting spiritual battles? I suppose by the time we've been a Christian for a few years, we've learned that we really can't afford to retire from fighting the devil without risking major shipwrecks in our lives. Even though this discovery might be terribly bothersome, we know we have no other choice if we want to make it to the end victoriously.

But there is one area in our Christian lives from which we can retire without obvious damage to our faith: the battle on behalf of others! It is definitely easier to retire than to keep fighting this battle.

How much effort is enough, we wonder, as we give of our time, strength, money, and intercession? The lost world is so vast that God cannot possibly mean that we take it all on our own shoulders for our entire life. For a little while, perhaps, we might, but surely not until we die. That would mess up all our plans and dreams for an easier life.

"Lord," we ask, "when can I shake off these burdens and

finally live in peace? Don't you agree that I deserve to enjoy my salvation, my family, and my church fellowship after all the work I have done for Your kingdom?"

In Hebrews 13:7, we are reminded to consider those who walked the path before us and to follow their faith and example. With this verse in mind, I want to share with you a little bit about Brother Thomas, one of the senior missionary leaders in India.

As a young man, Brother Thomas gave up everything to follow God's call to become a pioneer missionary in the state of Rajasthan, one of the most difficult areas for the Gospel in northern India. The tremendous suffering, persecution, and hardship he and his wife and a few co-workers went through during the past 35 years are impossible to describe.

Because of God's grace and Brother Thomas' faithfulness and leadership, today there is visible fruit of his ministry: 482 churches established, 75 mission schools, 14 orphanages, 11 Bible schools, seven radio programs in three languages, one mission hospital, six clinics, and church-planting work in 20 leper colonies.

Add to this the thousands of lives, including mine, who have been greatly influenced by this man's vision for God's kingdom, his love for the lost, and his example of faithfulness and endurance.

Several years ago, I received a letter from Brother Thomas that I would like to share with you. My sincere prayer is that his words will encourage and challenge you, as they did me, to continue to fight the battle on behalf of a lost world. Here is an excerpt from his letter:

> I was reading the book of Joshua during my daily devotions when the Lord particularly brought chapter 13, verse 1 to my attention: 'Now Joshua was old and stricken in years; and the LORD said unto him, Thou art old and stricken in years,

and there remaineth yet very much land to be possessed.'

Most of 1993 until now has been a time of continuous sickness in my life. It started with a cough and cold, until today even while I am writing this report, I am sick. I feel weak. When the Lord was speaking to Joshua after giving 31 kings and kingdoms into his hands, the Lord told him, 'It is true that you are old and stricken in years, but there remaineth very much land to be possessed!'

The Lord never gave Joshua any appreciation for acquiring these 31 kingdoms and destroying every individual in them, because it was not done by Joshua but by the Lord. Even now, to go back and possess more land for the Lord has nothing to do with the age of Joshua.

In the same way the Lord is able to give the land of India and its surrounding nations to us in spite of our sickness, weakness, and age. I praise God for this promise He has given to us.

Dear friend, if you ever feel the desire to retire from the battle on behalf of the lost world because you think you are too old, too tired, or not useful anymore, let me encourage you to remember those who have gone before you. Men like Moses, Joshua, and the apostle Paul also encountered the limitations of their physical bodies and mental strength. Yet they stayed in the battle until the end of their lives. Why? They had discovered, like Brother Thomas, that the Lord Himself is doing the fighting. All He looks for is a willing vessel through whom to work. It doesn't matter how fragile that vessel might be, because the battle is the Lord's and so is the victory.

Don't quit, stay in the battle.

Chapter 16

A Reason to Live

"You are trying to make us feel guilty," the woman protested loudly, interrupting the meeting of one of my staff members who was out sharing about the lost world and the work of the native missionaries.

"No," he assured her, "that is not my intent at all, but I believe God has put us here for a reason besides living for ourselves."

In my own travels, I often encounter similar situations. People get upset or defensive because they don't want to be disturbed in their comfort, the pursuit of their goals, and in living their peaceful lifestyles. To be confronted with the reality that 3.8 billion[1] unreached people will plunge into hell unless they receive a chance to hear the Gospel is irritating, troublesome, and uncomfortable to many believers. Why? Because their desire is to enjoy their salvation, families, church fellowships, seminars, and conferences without such a painful interruption.

When Jesus was telling the story about the rich man and Lazarus the beggar, He illustrated very clearly that the two had nothing to do with each other. The rich man was in his mansion enjoying the best of life, while the sick beggar was outside the gate hoping for a handout. It wasn't Lazarus' fault that there was no interaction between the two. He had

positioned himself strategically at the door where the rich
man could see him clearly every time he went in and out of
his gate. However, the rich man chose to ignore the beggar
for a very calculated reason. If he looked at Lazarus and the
dogs licking his sores, he wouldn't be able to enjoy his steak
dinner in peace!

What was his sin? He was selfish with his life and with all
God had entrusted to him.

Similarly, when the apostle Paul described to Timothy why
the last days would be so difficult, his number one reason
was: "For men will be lovers of themselves" (2 Timothy 3:2).

There is no statement that more accurately describes the
mindset of our present generation. We are constantly bom-
barded and counseled to be protective of ourselves, our possessions, our rights, and our wants. Everywhere we turn we
are told that we deserve the best. In fact, we are offered self-
help books and services on every conceivable subject.

What about the church? It is sad to say that this self-centered mindset has infiltrated much of the Body of Christ,
especially in more affluent countries. Our worship, our teaching, and our spiritual desires are primarily focused on, "Lord,
bless me, give to me, and let me enjoy."

Whatever happened to the war we are supposed to be in
and to the command: "And do not be conformed to this
world" (Romans 12:2)? Jesus taught us that the laws of the
kingdom of God are in sharp contrast with the mindset of
this world. For example, "For whoever desires to save his life
will lose it, and whoever will lose his life for My sake will
find it" (Matthew 16:25). We are fooling ourselves if we attempt to practice a Christianity without embracing the cross
and death to our own selves. Winning this world for Jesus
will never happen until we have the mind of Christ: "The
Son of Man did not come to be served, but to serve, and to
give His life a ransom for many" (Mark 10:45).

A few months ago while on the mission field, I met a

brother who has a death warrant on his life for preaching the Gospel. He has been imprisoned many times, beaten, stabbed, shot at, and on the run for months at a time. Yet he is eager to endure all these things in order to win one more soul to his Savior and King. "My life is nothing," he said. "It all belongs to Jesus." This brother has a wife and children who suffer alongside him—willingly. For them, Jesus is worth it all—the best reason to live.

Having the mind of Christ sets us free from our self-centeredness and enables us to minister to the Lazarus in front of our door!

How can we get that mind of Christ? Jesus gave the answer: "If anyone desires to come after Me, let him deny himself, and take up his cross daily, and follow Me" (Luke 9:23).

It starts with a deliberate decision to walk away from the mindset of self-preservation and allow the Lord to pour out our lives for the millions who have never before heard the name of Jesus.

The tragedy of the modern day church is that we have misunderstood obedience as legalism.

Chapter 17

"Lord, Break My Heart Afresh"

Even though I was on a crowded airplane high over my homeland of India, it took all the energy I had just to hold myself in the seat. Only moments before I had finished reading a shocking story on page one of a national newspaper. It pierced my heart with deep pain. It made me want to jump up and preach—to scream like one of the Old Testament prophets would—against the national sin of my people.

It was September of 1987, and India was still reeling in revulsion mixed with pride over the grotesque "sati" death of a teenage bride named Roop Kanwar in Rajasthan. Sati is an ancient Hindu religious practice in which a wife is burned alive on the funeral pyre of her husband.

In this instance, police stood helplessly by and watched the flames consume her living flesh before a crowd of 300,000 Hindu devotees. They were afraid of the fanatic mob. These Hindu pilgrims came from all over India to witness the ritual sacrifice of the 18-year-old girl.

Later, under pressure of public opinion from other parts of the country, family members were arrested for her murder. However, fanatic devotees declared that they planned to keep up their own pressure on the authorities until the organizers of the ritual killing were released.

What distressed me was that millions of my people were praising her religious devotion and saying, "We're finally getting back to being real Hindus!"

I shook my head in horror. "Can't they see the depravity of such a dark doctrine?" I asked myself over and over. "Who but the enemy of mankind could incite followers to such a fiery death?"

Sati was outlawed by the British at the instigation of William Carey, the modern pioneer of Christian missions in India. However, like the caste system, numerous evil rituals are still secretly practiced in many parts of the land. What shocked modern Indians of all religions is the fact that no attempt was made to keep this sati sacrifice secret. Police and government authorities were warned not to interfere because the sacrifice was a "religious affair."

In the past few years, "back to Hinduism" movements have become bolder and bolder in their militant demands for revival of ancient practices and suppression of other religions such as Christianity.

I used to hear the reports of this growing fanaticism yet remained untroubled. But God touched my heart on that plane, and I spent the rest of the flight crying out to God for India. I realized my need to pray and repent of the numbness I had allowed to grow in my conscience. I began asking God to break my heart afresh with the agony of the lost millions— people living in utter darkness.

Can you imagine the mindset of religions that allow and promote this kind of fanaticism? What is the fate of a nation whose people desire and glorify human sacrifice?

Since this last sati death, a lot of money was raised to erect a temple to honor Roop Kanwar, and devotional chants celebrating her "piety" have become popular.

As we read and hear these reports, we must pray that God

will tear our hearts and grip us with a genuine burden for these millions of lost souls. Bob Pierce, founder of World Vision International, once prayed, "Break my heart, Lord, with the things that break your heart."

Today, God is looking for those who will cry out that prayer **and** allow the Holy Spirit to take away our comfortable Christianity and totally transform our hearts. We need to let the Lord stamp a vision for eternity in our hearts and minds.

The situation in the subcontinent and throughout Asia is *not* hopeless. Christ is the answer. Millions will be freed from their bondage to darkness if only we will send messengers to them with the truth. The Word says, "For 'whoever calls on the name of the Lord shall be saved.' How then shall they call on Him in whom they have not believed? And how shall they believe in Him of whom they have not heard? And how shall they hear without a preacher? And how shall they preach unless they are sent?" (Romans 10:13-15).

Even if you personally cannot go to many of these nations in Asia, you still can make an impact. You can pray and be a *sender* of native missionaries, who will go and preach the Good News to those who have never heard. We are called to go *and* send to win the lost.

If your heart is stirred to do something to reach the most unreached in our generation, consider sponsoring a native missionary. You can write to the address on page 161 for more information.

If you truly desire to have a broken heart before God, I encourage you to pray this prayer, as I have for many years: "Lord, baptize me with desperation for souls."

Chapter 18

Walking into the Fire: Living on the Front Lines

While traveling in the Midwest, I was looking forward to meeting an old friend of mine. Years ago we had worked together on a Gospel team. I remember how I was challenged by his zeal for the Lord, his burden for the lost, and his example as a servant.

The more we talked, the more I realized he was no longer interested in reaching those who have never heard the Gospel. His whole life now revolved around his career and providing a more affluent lifestyle for his family. He had no more tears or passion for the lost. His reaction to everything I said about the mission field was cold and without enthusiasm. I returned to my hotel room that night, sadly wondering what had happened to my friend.

Thinking about my friend, I realized that the most difficult part of maintaining a radical walk with the Lord is not practicing a new lifestyle. It's not just mastering the basic teachings of the Bible or sharing our faith with others. It's not even praying effectively in faith for those in need or fighting the devil over public schools and politics.

The toughest challenge for believers today is to stay close to our Lord on the front lines, practically engaged in reaching the lost. When we first come to know the Lord or enlist in His army, we are so full of zeal and enthusiasm we can't wait to do combat.

However, as time goes by and we move from one battle to the next, we get weary. We wonder when the struggles will end. We discover that constant alertness and attack are exhausting.

We suddenly long for peace, relaxation, and early retirement. Most of us have no plans to quit the army altogether. We still want to serve, but no longer on the front lines where we are under constant attack.

Quitting the battle is not an overnight decision. It's a slow erosion of heart that often started long before. The shift is so subtle and gradual that we don't see it coming. When we discover our compromise, we try to defend and justify our position. But in reality we have already lost much of the love and commitment we once had for the Lord and His kingdom.

How did it all start? What was the root cause? How did we backslide, get sidetracked, quit the battle, and miss God's perfect will? What was the powerful temptation that overran our post?

Let me answer these questions with a quote I read recently that went something like this: None are more formidable instruments of temptation than well-meaning friends who care more for our comfort than for our character.

Whenever you decide to live radically committed to Christ and His call to win the lost, watch out! Immediately you will find well-meaning people rallying around you to help you stay "balanced." They're not your enemies—but your friends, your family members, and your brothers and sisters in the Body of Christ.

These people are truly concerned about your welfare. They give you heartfelt council: "Don't overdo it. Think about your future. What about your family? You have rights too. You will burn out. This can't be God's will for you. God never wants you to go overboard with this commitment. Think about your wife and children. You will regret it later."

The hardest decision you will ever have to make is to firmly tell those who love you, "I have decided to follow Jesus. Today I have put my hand to the plow and cannot look back. I have determined to give my life for the 3.8 billion[1] people who are unreached by the Gospel and are dying without Christ. Don't hold me back or feel sorry for me. My heart is fixed. Don't hold me back from pursuing the cross."

Unless you make a firm stand to choose Christ over comfort, you will sooner or later end up on the sidelines. The temptation to give in is powerful because of the relationship and love that bind you to these well-meaning people. Jesus knew this very well. That's why He told His disciples, "If anyone comes to Me and does not hate his father and mother, wife and children, brothers and sisters, yes, and his own life also, he cannot be My disciple. And whoever does not bear his cross and come after Me cannot be My disciple" (Luke 14:26-27).

Why do so many of our Christian brothers and sisters try to persuade us to seek our own comfort instead of laying down our lives? I believe the reason stems from a basic misunderstanding—they don't recognize that following Christ means to embrace the cross and, with it, death to our own self.

A careful study of Hebrews 11 reveals that everyone in the "hall of faith" paid a tremendously high price to be mentioned as our examples. Some left their countries, others high positions and riches. Many were persecuted, faced loneliness and rejection. A great number were beaten, killed, sawn apart, imprisoned, and burned alive. Yes, God rescued some of them to demonstrate His power, but many of them died at the front lines in the battle. The Bible says the world was not worthy of them.

When we look at the disciples and many of the Christians down through the centuries, we see thousands who died as martyrs while others suffered severe persecution for their faith. Paul's proof of his apostleship was not his "successes," but the price he paid for preaching the Gospel. His account in 2 Corinthians 11:23-28 lists scourging, imprisonments, beatings, a stoning, shipwrecks, and being betrayed by his own countrymen and false Christians. He could boldly say, "For our light affliction, which is but for a moment, is working for us a far more exceeding and eternal weight of glory" (2 Corinthians 4:17).

If we want to be serious about taking the Gospel to the 3.8 billion unreached people of our generation and the 80,000 who die every day without Christ, then we must come back to this kind of Christianity. We must be determined at all cost to stay on the front lines until Jesus comes back. We must encourage one another daily to reject the temptation of choosing comfort over Christ. We must walk into the fire of battle with everything we have, paying the price as Jesus did.

If we are determined to stay in the battle, we need to constantly examine everything we do in the light of eternity. Think about the lifestyle you have, the vacations you take, and the money you spend on yourself. What value do these things have in eternity? Do they help you maintain a broken heart for the lost world? If not, you need to make some changes. Consider one or more of the following:

•Set aside one day of the week for fasting and prayer for the unreached countries of the world. Read the book *Operation World* by Patrick Johnstone to help you know how to pray for specific nations.

•Be a bold witness to your co-workers at your job, the checkout lady at the supermarket, the man who sells you gasoline, and to people wherever you go.

•If you don't currently support a native missionary, decide to support one today.

Think about what extra "stuff" you could cut out of your budget to free up just $1 per day. Do something that counts!

"For what will it profit a man if he gains the whole world, and loses his own soul?" (Mark 8:36).

How many souls does it take to make our inconveniences worthwhile?

Chapter 19

Who Qualifies to Stand in the Gap?

It was by far the darkest hour in the history of the people of Israel. The lives of the entire nation were hanging by a very thin thread. At any moment, the judgment of their righteous God could wipe them off the face of the earth. They knew that each breath they took was only on borrowed time.

Frightened and trembling, the people stood at the foot of Mount Sinai, watching one old man slowly climb up the rough terrain to reach the top and meet the Holy God face-to-face. Moses' mission: to plead for mercy on behalf of several million people, to ask God to forgive their sin and continue to lead them to their promised land.

Moses himself must have felt the weight of the whole world on his shoulders. He knew God better than anyone alive. God couldn't simply forget His righteous standard and pretend the people's worship of the golden calf had never happened. He had to punish sin in accordance with His own character and His law, which demanded death for such a grave offense.

Considering all this, why did Moses even try to make this

tiring hike and approach God in such a hopeless situation? I believe he must have said to himself: "I have no doubt that because the people have broken their covenant with God, He must punish them. But from all my previous encounters with Him, I have learned that He is also a merciful God who dearly loves His people. Perhaps there is a chance He will spare them if I stand in the gap for them."

Chapter 32 of the book of Exodus contains the dialogue between God and Moses on Mount Sinai. The first part of their conversation had taken place when God gave Moses the tablets with the commandments and informed him of the idol worship that was going on in the camp of Israel. The second half happened after Moses went down to see for himself, smashed the tablets in the process, destroyed the golden calf, and then came back up the mountain to plead for the lives of his people.

Here we see Moses standing in the breach of a broken dam, fighting to hold off the imminent flood of destruction that is about to wipe out an entire nation. Imagine with me, if you will, their conversation: God says, "Moses, step aside and let Me destroy them. They have gone too far—there is no hope for them. I will raise you up as a new nation instead, and your descendants will be My people." But Moses simply answers, "Please, God, You cannot do that. These are Your people. You are the One who led them out of Egypt. If You are going to destroy them, then please kill me also. Wipe my name out of Your book."

God heard Moses' prayer as he pleaded for millions of people who had walked away from the living God. Amazing! His standing in the gap allowed the entire nation of Israel to be saved.

What was it that compelled God to listen to Moses? Why did God accept him and grant his request? God looked at Moses' heart, and He saw a man who was totally unselfish in all his ways. His heart was pure. His motives were without hidden agendas. God could say this about him: "Moses, My servant, with whom I share all My secrets." He walked with God in such a way that he could go up the mountain and sit and talk with God, and then go down and speak to the people. He was able to identify with them yet at the same time remain God's faithful servant.

We can learn a valuable lesson from Moses' life. When souls are hanging in the balance, it is not the majority of the crowd that will make the difference. All God needs and looks for is one individual whose heart is pure. My brothers and sisters, this means you and I can make the difference in our home, our workplace, our community, our state, and our nation. Please believe me, we can—if our hearts are right.

The history of the nation of Israel is marked by terrible times of judgment, devastation, and exile, yet there is always the hope of God's promise—that He will not wipe them out completely and will show them mercy if they seek Him again.

When we read the Old Testament, we encounter a God who takes no pleasure in judging and punishing His people for their rebellion and sin. On the contrary, He is deeply grieved; and He actually looks for a reason to keep from having to go through with His judgment. In Ezekiel 22:30, we see the pain and sadness of His heart when He tells us through the prophet: "So I sought for a man among them who would make a wall, and stand in the gap before Me on behalf of the land, that I should not destroy it; but I found no one."

The background to this verse is this: God's people—the entire nation—had forsaken the living God. They were totally given over to idolatry, corruption, self-centered living, greed, lust, and seeking after the things of this world. God was deeply grieved over His beloved people. He knew He would have to send His severe judgment and wipe them out. But in the middle of all this chaos, He must have paused and remembered Mount Sinai, and how Moses selflessly stood in the gap and saved his people. Right then, in His love and desire to find a way to ward off judgment, God must have decided: "I will look for just one individual—not 10, 15, or 10,000—with a heart like Moses', whose intercession I can accept; one, among all my people, who is honest with total integrity, who has a deep concern for others and is pure in his intentions, who will stand in the gap on their behalf and pray and plead for their lives. I will carefully search through the entire nation, among the thousands of priests, prophets, and people who declare they belong to Me and work for My cause."

God made the most thorough search ever conducted on the face of the earth, but He came up empty-handed. "I found none," He lamented, and the land was destroyed and the people killed or taken away into exile.

Why was there no one at all who could have stood in the gap for God's people? At least among the priests and Levites there should have been someone who qualified. Were God's standards higher than in Moses' time? No, not at all. But something very alarming had happened in the lives and ministries of those priests and Levites who had been specifically appointed by God to teach and lead His people according to His Word. In Ezekiel 22:26, God describes very clearly why the spiritual corrosion among the nation was so total: "Her priests have violated My law and profaned My holy things; they have not distinguished between the holy and unholy, nor have they made known the difference between the unclean and the clean...."

When I read these words, they really spoke to my heart. I want to draw your attention to the part of Ezekiel 22:26 where God says, "They have not distinguished between the holy and the unholy." This particular verse is interestingly paraphrased in the Living Bible: "Your priests have violated my laws and defiled my Temple and my holiness. To them the things of

God are no more important than any daily task."

Incredible! Among these thousands of priests and prophets, God could not find one person—even though every one of them was busy in ministry. What were these people doing? What was their problem? God says, "They took the ministry lightly and treated My work just like any other secular job. They lost the heart of the whole thing!"

The motive behind each action is what gives the action its value. The motive behind your service, your prayers, your toil—whatever you do—is what the Lord examines and evaluates. Your work may be minimal, or it may be a sleepless, 24-hour job. No matter what it is, the reason you do it is so much more important, in God's eyes, than what you actually do. In other words, the question "why" is far more crucial than the question "what."

Over the years I have watched Gospel for Asia expand to many countries and touch the lives of millions of people. All the while, this one burden and longing continues to grow in my own heart: "Lord, create in us a deeper reality. Make us authentic in our hearts, that we will be pure before You."

You see, authenticity is what it takes to stand in the gap for a lost world and to do a work for God that will last throughout eternity. Otherwise, we will only end up with a huge pile of wood, hay, and stubble that will be burned up into just a pinch of ash.

Do you remember how strongly and angrily Jesus spoke to the Pharisees and scribes of His day? These people were believed to be righteous and holy because externally, they did everything perfect: they fasted, prayed, memorized the law of Moses, and taught the Holy Scriptures. In fact, these men were scholars—the equivalent of Ph.D.'s in theology. They were employed full-time in the work of God. Everything else in life was secondary. Their total lifetime commitment was to God and His law and to the task of teaching and practicing it.

But you know what? Jesus pronounced His worst judgment,

not on the prostitutes, drunkards and the most wicked crooks in this society, but on this religious crowd. His words to them in Matthew 23:27, 33 are extremely strong: "Woe to you, scribes and Pharisees, hypocrites! For you are like whitewashed tombs which indeed appear beautiful outwardly, but inside are full of dead men's bones, and all uncleanness. . . . Serpents, brood of vipers! How can you escape the condemnation of hell?"

Why did Jesus deal so severely with them? What was their problem? They did everything so correctly and according to all the rules and regulations. But Jesus was not looking at their outside deeds, but at the "why"—the motives of their hearts. What He saw there was the exact same problem what occurred as in the days of Ezekiel: They served God with an external form, but their heart was not in it. And thus they disqualified themselves from being used by God to stand in the gap for the people.

What about us as New Testament believers? What is our track record with the living God? We can boast of thousands of impressive churches and accomplishments in the name of Christ, and many of our preachers and evangelists have huge followings. But how would we fare as individuals, if God would evaluate us by the same criteria He used in Moses' and Ezekiel's days? Would we qualify to stand in the gap for those who are about to be destroyed and plunged into hell?

Jesus had much to say about the heart motives of those who claim to be His followers. In fact, in Matthew 7:22-23, He described a scene from the future, the Day of Judgment: "Many will say to Me in that day, 'Lord, Lord, have we not prophesied in Your name, cast out demons in Your name and done many wonders in Your name?' And then I will declare to them, 'I never knew you; depart from Me, you who practice lawlessness!'"

This is a very sobering passage of Scripture. Imagine for a moment how sad and terrified these people will feel as they cry out in desperation, "Jesus, You somehow must have made a mistake! Don't You remember me? I'm the one who saw thousands of people healed in my ministry. Demons trembled and left people when I commanded them to get out in the name of Jesus. And Lord, how many thousands made decisions for You at my evangelistic meetings?"

Amazingly, Jesus doesn't reply, "No, you're lying. You didn't do any of these things." In fact, He makes no comment at all about the subject they used for their defense. His silence about the whole matter of their ministry accomplishments is proof and declaration that they did perform all those miracles and works.

But then Jesus very plainly tells them, without further explanation or qualification: "I never knew you; depart from Me, you who practice lawlessness!"

Let me ask you, how did such an incredible amount of spiritual Christian work, which received the applause of the whole world and drew enormous crowds, turn out in the end to be "works of iniquity"?

I believe the answer is this: Those workers did all their ministry not for the glory of God, but for their own name, their benefit, man's approval, and man's honor. Their motivation and reason for serving God were carnal, and in the depth of their heart their intentions were impure.

My brothers and sisters, I know these are very strong statements. For all of us who desire to serve the Lord and are committed to reach our generation with the Gospel, my deepest concern is that we have a pure and authentic heart before the Lord. We must never work and serve because of a challenge, money, a title, a position, or even because millions of people are going to hell and we have to do something about it. It is my prayer and hope that we serve the living God for one reason, and no other: deep down in our hearts, we love Jesus more than anything else in this life, and His love is our only motivation for action.

Only those things done out of sincere love will last in eternity.

Chapter 20

A Major Trap

Recently, one of Gospel for Asia's missionary training centers faced serious trouble from anti-Christian authorities in a neighboring country. A number of the people in a border region of that country had accepted Jesus through the witness of our students. The school received a letter with an order to close down immediately.

In every country where Gospel for Asia works, our native missionaries, staff and friends prayed earnestly for God to intervene. The decision was reversed a week later, and the school was allowed to remain open. Praise God for His wonderful answer to prayer.

If I could pick out one thing that Jesus—as well as Paul and the rest of the apostles—constantly emphasized, it would be prayer. In the Scriptures, we are charged to "watch and pray," to "pray without ceasing," that "intercessions . . . be made for all men," and so on.

Most followers of Christ are convinced that prayer is a vital part of our Christian life. Through prayer, we communicate with God. As we petition Him, in His love He meets our needs, heals our sicknesses, and delivers us from Satan's attacks. In fact, we know from Scripture that prayer is our mightiest weapon to defeat the enemy. As we pray, all heaven fights for us.

Amazingly, despite our vast knowledge about the

importance of prayer, we struggle constantly to find time for it. Prayer usually ends up near the bottom of our priority list.

There is a reason for this! You see, the devil hates prayer. He hates it more than choir practice, seminars, conferences, and Christian concerts. He will do everything in his power to stop us from engaging in this dangerous activity. In fact, prayer is so destructive to him that he is more than happy to see us choose instead to listen to a sermon, read a Christian book, or work for charity.

However, if the devil can't hinder us from praying, he uses several other effective tactics to zap the power out of our prayers. One of those tactics is this: without us knowing, he slips in slowly and makes us believe that all these great victories have happened because of *us* and *our* prayers. For example, this endangered training center was saved because "we" knew how to defeat the devil. The radio broadcast received 10,000 letters this month because *we* made it happen through *our* intercession.

Unless we are very careful and extremely sensitive, we can end up at a place where even our prayers can become a major trap. You see, when things are happening, the enemy tempts us to trust in *our* prayer activity, *our* expertise on spiritual warfare, *our* elite group, and *our* dynamite church leadership. Suddenly our confidence is placed in ourselves and what we are able to accomplish instead of in the Lord alone. Thus, our prayers have turned into a work of the flesh, something God detests and always rejects.

On every page of the Bible, we see a battle between the flesh and the Spirit. God clearly demonstrates and proves throughout history that no product of the flesh is accepted or receives any glory. We have a good example of this in the life of Abraham.

Abraham's entire struggle was to learn to quit placing his confidence in his own flesh and his ability to father the promised son. When he trusted in his flesh, he produced Ishmael instead of Isaac. With great hopes he brought Ishmael to God, asking Him to bless his son. The Lord looked at Abraham, and (to paraphrase) He said, "You can pray a thousand years, Abraham, and it will change nothing. I had nothing to do with producing this child. It's your own work. He looks real and is absolutely healthy, vibrant, and strong. He talks, walks, moves, and jumps. But if you look behind the story of Ishmael's conception, you will not find Me there."

God had to bring Abraham and his wife, Sarah, to a point in their lives where there was no hope left whatsoever. It was then that God commanded Abraham to be circumcised. This was Abraham's testimony that he no longer had any confidence in his flesh. God became his only hope for receiving his promised son. And that's when Isaac was born.

Our prayers and intercession are vitally important to reach the lost world. There is no substitute for pulling down the strongholds of the enemy. Therefore, we must keep our weapon of prayer sharp and effective at all times, which happens only when we examine our hearts daily to see if we are placing our confidence in anything other than Jesus alone. God seeks followers and intercessors who believe with all their hearts that it is "not by might, nor by power, but by My Spirit, says the LORD of hosts" (Zechariah 4:6).

A few minutes of prayer with total dependence on the Lord are worth more than days of weeping in our own strength. Don't forget the priorities. We may cry out all day long and see nothing happen, yet Elijah prayed a few words and fire came down from heaven!

When will we ever learn?

Chapter 21

Don't Look for Peace

As followers of Christ, we very often forget that we are engaged in a serious battle with bullets flying all around us. Just recently I counseled a Christian leader in India who was deeply discouraged because of the sudden pressures he was facing in his ministry. Some years ago, this man had graduated with top honors from engineering school and was employed in Nigeria. He had plenty of money, a huge house, and everything else he could wish for in life. One day his father, just prior to death, wrote him a letter, which ended by saying, "Son, remember you have only one life. It will soon be gone. Make a decision how you will invest your life."

The last sentence of his father's letter caused him to resign from his job and leave everything to follow Christ's call and give his life to serve the Lord full time. He began to recruit young people, train them at a small Bible school he started, and send them out to mission fields in northern India.

They all were serving the Lord quite well and his ministry was growing when he came to me so downtrodden. I was a bit surprised to see this brother in such despair—wanting to give up the ministry and run away from the community in which he was working—and ready to fall to pieces. I wondered what had happened to him. He is known as a man with great understanding of the Lord and His Word, and he has a deep walk with God.

So I sat down and listened to his story. This is what he said:

"My wife and I and our children gave up everything we had to serve the Lord. We held nothing back. Now I am facing misunderstandings with my co-workers and criticism from other people. I don't know what to do, and I can't take it anymore."

I patiently listened and let him cry about all the terrible things that had happened to him. To me a lot of them seemed insignificant, but he was being destroyed by them.

In the end I said to him, "Brother, let me tell you an instant solution to all your problems. If you follow my advice, I guarantee you total recovery from criticism, problems, misunderstanding, and even the sickness you are facing." His face lit up, and he was eager to hear my solution.

"Brother," I continued, "go home and tell your wife and children that you are getting out of the ministry and that you might go back to engineering or join an organization that doesn't get involved with the front line battlefield."

What I said visibly shook him up. He had not expected this kind of solution.

"I am not joking with you," I said. "I am dead serious. Tell me, did you have any of these problems before you walked away from engineering?"

"No," he answered. "I had a mansion, servants, cars, and everything was going great."

"Brother," I said, "now your life is all messed up and you are being destroyed. This is cause and effect. The reason you are having all these difficulties is because you are actively fighting against the kingdom of darkness. The apostle Paul was engaged in this same warfare and look what he faced."

I opened the Bible to 2 Corinthians 11:23-28 and showed him the list Paul made about his sufferings on behalf of the Gospel. He was shipwrecked, beaten, forsaken by all, near death, hungry, misunderstood, and so on. I told him the best way to get away from all these troubles was to stay home or do something besides pioneer evangelism. "However, if you want to serve the Lord, you don't have many choices. You will not only face your present difficulties, but all of them will be multiplied a thousand times in the days to come. Perhaps you will even face an early death. But that is what Jesus promised. Will you accept it?" I asked.

I prayed and encouraged him, and he went back to his home. Before I left India, he sent somebody to tell me that his life was completely turned around. Now he is not expecting an easy road. He is fully expecting service to the Lord to be a battle and a struggle.

I myself needed that same encouragement when I was "down" some years ago. At that time I called Brother Alfy Franks, one of the senior Operation Mobilization leaders in India, and told him that I was in bad shape. This is what he told me, "I'll tell you what your problem is. You are looking for peace. When you are working in front line evangelism, you never get out of the fight. You get into one battle; and as soon as it is over, you get into a new one. This is a nonstop war, especially when we are involved in reaching the lost world."

Since that talk with Brother Alfy, I have never again looked for peace or for a time when I could say, "Oh wonderful, everything is going great." No, I am prepared for battle and for staying in the fight. I get wounded sometimes and discouraged. All of us do. This is normal in a battle!

But like Paul we can say: "We are hard pressed on every side, yet not crushed; we are perplexed, but not in despair; persecuted, but not forsaken; struck down, but not destroyed" (2 Corinthians 4:8-9). In the end after the battle is over, we will still be standing and going forward. That is God's promise.

This is not fatalism. No, we are more than conquerors through Him who loved us. So by life or death we serve Him, knowing that He is our victory.

You are not your own—remember that blood was the price Jesus paid for you!

Chapter 22

What Is Normal?

Many years ago, my oldest brother came to know the Lord in a very intimate way. At that time my mother was a believer, but the rest of our family wasn't saved. One day my brother read the promise in Acts 16:31, "Believe on the Lord Jesus Christ, and you will be saved, you and your household." The message of this verse went deep into his heart. As he read it, the Holy Spirit touched his spirit, and he said, "If this is what God said, it must be so! I will believe it."

From that day on my brother began to pray for everyone's salvation, believing that his family was already saved. One by one, our entire family came to know the Lord. Their children were also saved, and most of our extended family was saved as well. In fact, many of our family members are either in full-time ministry or in preparation for it.

It was only many years later that I realized what my brother had understood was the mystery of walking by faith described in Hebrews 11:1. Unfortunately, many Christians do not have this kind of trusting faith.

I believe the devil laughs when he sees us sitting down with our calculators, logic and expertise to figure a way out of our problems and battles. He knows very well that even if we held 10 Ph.D.s, we couldn't outsmart him. I imagine he actually enjoys watching us depend on our great knowledge, the latest management strategies, and human psychology to run our churches, evangelize the world, and heal our ills. You see, as long as he can keep us believing that we can find answers and solutions in the realm of the natural, we are not much of a threat to him.

God, on the other hand, urges us to live in the supernatural. This means walking by faith and believing His Word, even if it defies everything our five senses tell us.

Faith has nothing to do with human logic, mathematics, or what we can see, hear, feel, smell, or touch. But it has everything to do with how God operates! Faith disregards the obvious facts and trusts that God will do the impossible. The Bible clearly demonstrates that God requires this kind of faith from His people:

• "Moses, stretch your rod over the Red Sea, and it will part."

• "Joshua, march with your army around Jericho for seven days, and the walls will crumble."

• "David, go to war against Goliath with a sling and a stone, and you will kill him and deliver your people."

• "Bartimaeus, call out to the Son of David, and He will open your blind eyes."

• "Woman, touch the hem of His garment, and you will be healed."

• "Father, bring your son to Jesus, and He will deliver him from the demon."

• "Martha, if you believe, you will see the glory of God and Lazarus will live."

Hebrews 11:1 says, "Now faith is the substance of things hoped for, the evidence of things not seen," meaning that when I walk by faith, I believe without a shadow of a doubt that God's promise to me is the absolute truth. I then act and live at that very moment—before I ever see the evidence—as if I have already received the fulfillment. If I do this, the Bible declares that I will have my request.

To our human logic it sounds as if God wants us to lie about our real situation. It sounds so foolish, so opposite of reality, and so unscientific! But according to Hebrews 11:1, we are not lying at all; and we haven't fallen into a trap of hopeless self-deception. No, we are just acting normally—by the laws that govern heaven!

None of this makes sense to our human perception. It blows our minds just trying to figure it out.

The most important thing for us to remember is this: it is impossible to apply the laws of the natural realm to the realm of the supernatural.

Jesus said in John 17:14 that we are not of this world, just as He is not of this world. We are born of the Spirit of God and belong to another kingdom that is not a part of this earth. For us as citizens of heaven, it should be only normal that we live according to the laws of our home world!

Perhaps some of us are reluctant to enter such a walk of faith as described in Hebrews 11:1. We have seen a lot of fraud with a pretense of faith, and it has scared us off.

True faith has nothing to do with lies, foolishness, manipulation, and claiming wild things God never intended for us to have. True faith first receives a clear promise of God that is within His revealed will and then acts on it.

Once we have determined to walk by faith, we will encounter severe opposition from the devil. In fact, our greatest battle will take place between the time we decide to believe God's promise and the actual, visible moment of fulfillment.

That's the time the enemy fights the most. He attacks our mind and tells us, "What kind of a fool are you to believe God would heal your sickness, restore your marriage, save your son, or provide for your needs? It's already been three weeks since you decided to pray by faith. Take a look at your situation. Has it changed? Nothing has happened—nothing at all!

"How long do you want to continue deceiving yourself? You are way off course with your religion. Even if God does such miracles for others, what makes you think He would do them for you? Just look at you. You are not good enough to qualify. You don't even pray enough. . . ."

Satan tries his best to discourage us with all these doubts. He wants us to give up walking by faith and consequently never see the fulfillment of God's promise to us. We must resist the devil and his attack on our minds, and he will flee from us.

As we continually walk by faith and not by sight, we live in the supernatural. God's very life flows through us unhindered, and we become a mighty weapon in His hand. He is now able to use us to bring millions of people to Jesus, change the course of nations, and proclaim His kingdom on earth.

All things are possible if only you believe.

Chapter 23

Does Your Reading Count?

While visiting China a while back, I was shocked when I learned that hundreds of church congregations there are without even one copy of the Bible to share among themselves. They are without any kind of Christian book, and still in many parts of the world it is impossible to find a Christian bookstore.

In free countries, especially in the West, thousands of books on every conceivable subject are available to believers. One might logically conclude that because there are so many Christian books, most of the people in these nations are very spiritual and radical in their commitment to Christ!

Unfortunately, this is not the case. In fact, even though so many Christian books are available, many of God's people are truly illiterate when it comes to reading books that could really make a difference in their lives. When you visit the average Christian bookstore, you'll find that there are more books on self-help and how to make one feel good or how to improve one's situation, than on the radical call of Christ to lay down one's life and live unselfishly to reach this generation with the Gospel.

Many publishing houses will not publish a book with the name "mission" on it, simply because it wouldn't be a money maker. Furthermore, hundreds of priceless books are out of print because the topics are contrary to our self-centered, self-pleasing, watered-down Christianity. And do you realize the latest trend is to read Christian novels? In other words, we are looking for anything that makes us feel good.

Early in my Christian life, one of the best things that happened to me was that George Verwer, founder of Operation Mobilization, at which I was serving, asked us young people to carry with us the book *True Discipleship*, by William McDonald. He wanted us to read it several times each year. Then I was introduced to the many books by A. W. Tozer and by Watchman Nee. And, of course, one cannot forget the book *Calvary Road* by Roy Hession. I'm sad to say that many of these books are not even available in the most popular bookstores. They have to be special ordered.

Read the Gospels and see how Jesus called His disciples. He said, "If anyone desires to come after Me, let him deny himself, and take up his cross, and follow Me" (Matthew 16:24). And, "If anyone comes to Me, and does not hate his father and mother, wife and children, brothers and sisters, yes, and his own life also, he cannot be My disciple" (Luke 14:26). Of course, Jesus promised a hundredfold more blessings than anything we can ever forsake. But He said these blessings would also come with much persecution.

There is a price to pay in this generation if we are serious about seeing the multiplied millions of people in this world come to know the Lord Jesus Christ. We are truly in serious spiritual warfare. Satan is serious not only about what he is doing but also about drugging us with this lukewarm Christianity and plunging us in a fog that blinds us to reality.

I encourage you to get some of the books I mentioned previously. Read them and meditate on them. Then read the Gospels and let the Lord speak to you in a fresh and new way.

Next, pray. There is no greater test of a person's grasp on reality than seeing how he is committed to prayer. How can we watch 139,000 people being wiped away in a cyclone in Bangladesh, 50,000 slaughtered in Sri Lanka, or hundreds killed on the streets in China and then take it so casually? If Christ were there in the flesh to witness these events, how would He react? I believe His heart would be breaking, and food, sleep, hobbies, and anything else that might be considered important would become secondary. Would Jesus not fall down weeping and praying? Isn't this what we ought to be doing? I believe the daily events happening in the world should become a prayer letter we can use to intercede for this generation.

As you think about getting some of these excellent books, I would also recommend *Operation World*, by Patrick Johnstone. It is a must, because it gives the reader information on how to pray for each country. If you are unable to get any of the books I've mentioned in your bookstores, please let Gospel for Asia know. We may be able to help you locate them.

Read not just for information, but to learn and obey.

Chapter 24

Somewhere Down the Road

It was an exciting day for the Christians in Antioch. The whole church had gathered together to pray for Paul and to send him off on his second missionary journey.

Everybody was curious to see who would be on his team this time. You see, just a few days before there had been quite a heated dispute between Paul and Barnabas, who had accompanied Paul on his first trip. Barnabas wanted John Mark to join them again so the young man could have a second chance as a missionary candidate. On the last trip, he had deserted them when things got rough, but Barnabas believed that John Mark had now changed and would do better.

But Paul's list of qualifications to serve on his elite team didn't include such generosity! In fact, if Paul had lived in our days, the advertisement he might have published in Christian magazines would read something like the following:

Team Members Wanted for Mission Work in Asia Minor and Europe
1. Job description: Serving, praying, preaching, teaching, and church planting.

2. Qualification: Love Jesus more than life itself.

3. Terms and conditions: Hard work; 24-hour shifts; difficult travel; storms; ship wrecks; nakedness; poverty; hunger; constant danger from Gentiles, false brothers, robbers, and wild animals; misunderstanding; loneliness; desertion by co-workers; persecution; beatings; stonings; imprisonment; and possible martyrdom.

4. Job doesn't include the following benefits: Salary, position, title, promotion, securities, health or life insurance, secure future, good health, long life, and retirement fund.

Please send your application to Paul of Tarsus, apostle to the Gentiles.

I am certain that very few of us would have dared to venture out and join Paul's "death squad" missionary team! In fact, most of our comfort-loving churches would have labeled Paul as crazy, dangerous, and cultish and warned their members not to attend his meetings or read his letters.

However, when we read the Gospels, we are surprised to discover that Jesus made the same offer to His disciples when He asked them to follow Him. He even told them, "You must love Me more than your own life." We read the results in the book of Acts and in church history: nearly all of His disciples lost their lives for the sake of the Gospel they preached.

On that day when Paul headed out for his second missionary journey, "a few good men" had actually made his team! Everyone in the church knew that these men had to be the cream of the crop, the best of Christianity: men full of faith and the Holy Spirit, mavericks, steadfast, fearless, and invincible.

Paul and his team were incredibly successful. Everywhere they went, they drew people's attention with the message they preached and the miracles God performed through them. People were saved, churches were established, and together, this team actually turned the known world upside-down (see Acts 17:6).

Years later, however, Paul wrote an interesting paragraph in his letter to the Philippian church. "But I hope in the Lord Jesus to send Timothy to you shortly, so that I also may be encouraged when I learn of your condition. For I have no one else of kindred spirit who will genuinely be concerned for your welfare. For they all seek after their own interests, not those of Christ Jesus. But you know of his proven worth that he served with me in the furtherance of the gospel like a child serving his father" (Philippians 2:19-22, NASB).

And with sorrow, Paul wrote to Timothy at the end of his life: "Demas has forsaken me, having loved this present world, and has departed for Thessalonica" (2 Timothy 4:10).

What strange things is Paul writing about in these letters? He's actually talking about his own co-workers! How is that possible? What happened to his elite team, the ones he hand-picked and personally trained?

In the beginning, it was fantastic how everyone worked hard and gladly sacrificed and suffered together. No one asked for a title or claimed a position. Each one was eager to serve Paul and the other team members. But as time went by, something shifted in their hearts. They became secretly concerned about their own career as Gospel workers. One after another, each man said to himself: "I love the Lord , the ministry, and Paul, but if I go on working for Paul, I'll miss my chance to build my own ministry and make a name for myself."

Many left Paul and his team for various reasons. Paul was sad and hurt, not because he didn't want his co-workers to be used by God elsewhere but because he recognized that the motivation of their hearts had changed. The driving factor in their ministry decision was no longer love for Jesus but rather their own interests, dreams, and ambitions.

In the Old Testament, we find another example of a man being motivated by his own interests and desires. Gehazi, the servant of the prophet Elisha, had stood with his master through difficult and turbulent times. He had traveled with Elisha, carried his bags, cooked his food, and shared all the hardships and persecution Elisha faced in his ministry. It was not an easy life for Gehazi. Surely no one envied him for his job.

I believe Gehazi had originally joined up with Elisha because of his love for the God of Israel and because he truly believed Elisha was a genuine prophet of the Lord. He saw it as a special privilege and honor to serve such a man and help make his life a little easier.

For his part, Elisha might have looked at Gehazi as a gift of God to his ministry. Perhaps he even thought: "Could it be that God has sent Gehazi to live with me because He is preparing him to be the next prophet for Israel after I am gone? After all, Moses' long-time servant Joshua became his successor; and I myself used to be Elijah's servant."

Gehazi worked hard and seemed faithful in his service. . . until Naaman, captain of the Syrian army, showed up and offered Elisha riches out of gratitude for curing his leprosy. But when Elisha refused to accept the goods and Gehazi watched Naaman and his treasures disappear down the road, he panicked. I imagine he thought something like this: "How could Elisha do this? If he didn't want any gifts, that's his choice. But he could have thought about me just this once, and let me have a little reward. I have nothing to show for all my years of faithful service. Unless I act quickly, I will lose the chance of a lifetime to get something for myself!"

So Gehazi ran after Naaman, got some free gold and clothing . . . and became a leper.

This is a very sad story. We can't help but wonder how Gehazi could make such a fatal mistake after being with Elisha for so long. Surely he must have known that he would never get away with this type of greed.

Was Gehazi perhaps always a selfish man and served the prophet only for a chance like this? Or could it be that his heart went from a state of total commitment to seeking his own benefit in just a matter of hours?

I believe Gehazi actually started out with the right motivation, but somewhere down the road, his heart was lost, long before he encountered Naaman.

Is it that God doesn't want us to have any blessings as we live for Him and serve Him? No, not at all! On the contrary, He is eager to shower us with His goodness. But He doesn't want us to make the blessings and benefits our goal and reason for service. He knows that if we do, we will lose the purity of our motivation, which should be to serve Him out of love.

A third example is found in the church in Ephesus, which Paul himself planted. This church was a model to all of Christianity: genuine love for Jesus, commitment, maturity, sacrifice, and hard work. When Paul wrote them a letter, he didn't have to spend time reteaching them the spiritual ABCs, but instead could share deep spiritual truths with them.

But years later, another letter reached the Ephesians from the apostle John, with a message he had received from Jesus. The content was very short but extremely serious, in essence it said: I know all you do—your work is way above average. However, you have lost your first love, and there is nothing I can accept as a substitute. Repent, and love Me as you did in the beginning. If not, I will walk out of your church (see Revelation 2:2-5).

It is shocking, but when we study about Paul's co-workers, Gehazi, and the church in Ephesus, we find the same problem. The beginning of their ministry was wonderful.

Their hearts were right, and their motives were pure. But as time went by and their knowledge of God, their experience in ministry, and their ability to lead others all increased, their hearts changed.

Their problem—and ours as well—was not the start of the race but that long stretch before the finish line. Looking at those who have gone before us, we can easily see that this is where we face our greatest battles and where so many fail. Perhaps with time, we become more casual and careless and take much of our walk with the Lord and our ministry for granted.

Paul, on the other hand, ran the race and kept his faith and motivation intact until the end of his life. Time did not seem to affect him. What did he do to live victoriously until the end? I am very sure he applied Proverbs 4:23 literally to his life: "Keep your heart with all diligence, for out of it spring the issues of life."

Paul watched over his heart with the eyes of an eagle, alert and ready to detect any early warning signs that he was losing his pure motivation. If this started to happen he immediately corrected his course.

Above all, Paul never considered himself more than a bondservant or slave of Jesus Christ. As such, he had laid down every right to his own life along with every ambition he ever had. His only remaining desire was to please His Lord and live for Him. He entertained no dreams beyond that.

In the light of all this, seeking recognition, titles, position, a pat on the back, salary, or benefits in the Lord's work, whether secretly or openly, must be an alarming warning sign for us. If we choose to pursue these things, it will be only a matter of time before we have lost a pure motivation of the heart.

Our enemy is our own self-centeredness.

Chapter 25

Are We Seeing Through the Eyes of Jesus?

Things aren't always as they appear to us at first glance. It's true, isn't it? Let me explain what I mean: you make a phone call to an old friend just to say hello, but he responds with harsh words and shows no interest in talking with you. By the time you hang up, you are convinced he is upset with you. A week later, you find out that his wife was diagnosed with cancer just hours before you made your phone call. The situation was not at all as it appeared, and you had to revise your earlier judgment.

How easily we judge others every day, without actually knowing the full story! In the book of Samuel, we read the story of Hannah, a lonely, heartbroken woman who came to the temple to pour her soul out before the Lord. In her pain and heaviness of heart, she wept bitterly and could barely utter a few words in prayer. The priest Eli, who watched from a distance, only saw her lips tremble as she sobbed her request to God . . . and he promptly accused her of being drunk. When she explained her story, Eli no longer condemned her, but with a heart of compassion he blessed her in the name of Jehovah.

Eli made the mistake of basing his quick judgment of Hannah on her outward appearance. God corrected him by making him look at her heart and take time to listen to her whole story.

What Eli did is exactly what we do to others: we pass judgment without knowing the real condition or situation, and we end up condemning others. Furthermore, we often use harsh, sarcastic words and expressions in our "verdict" and end up hurting others deeply. Although they may respond to our sarcasm with a smile, deep down in their heart they are weeping. We must never forget that when we carelessly hurt the least of our brothers and sisters, we are hurting the Lord Himself.

Why is our perception of others and their problems often so inaccurate and insensitive, even if we consider all the facts? Because we lack God's perspective on their situation. As human beings, we are so limited in our ability to understand one another. We don't see the world through the eyes of our fellow man, but only through our own. Subsequently, our own experience, traditions, and values are the measuring scale for our judgment and the reality we perceive in the world around us. If we use ourselves and our circumstantial views of reality as final authorities for assessing others, we will inevitably make hopeless and inaccurate judgments.

Because each person on earth lives and judges by his own perception of reality, how can we ever respond to a situation in the right way? We can't . . . until we recognize that God alone is the measuring scale for all things and that without the guidance of the Holy Spirit we are incapable of discerning the hearts of men, their true needs, and God's answer for their situations. In other words, we must learn to see others through the eyes of Jesus.

The story of Peter in the 10th chapter of Acts is a classic example of how Peter's view of reality, which was created by his upbringing, traditions, and convictions, became a major hindrance to his ability to do God's will. Being a Jew, he could have no dealings whatsoever with Gentiles. But here we see Peter throwing out his lifelong judgment on Gentiles and traveling to the house of Cornelius to lead him and his entire family to Christ. What happened to Peter? He allowed the Holy Spirit to replace his own faulty conception of reality with God's perfect one; and as a result, he was able to respond as Jesus would.

I believe the most disturbing reason we are so quick to judge others is our deep-seated pride. We don't want to admit it, but we often secretly delight in their flaws and problems. Their failures give us something to talk about and at the same time make us look holy. In reality, our hearts are so wicked that we actually feel elevated when someone else falls! If we could see them with the eyes of Jesus, we would intercede with tears for their restoration.

Do we judge the motives of others? This is one of the worst things we can do. Without even asking one question, we make up our mind and say things like, "I know why he is saying this or why she is doing that." When we do this, we seat ourselves on the throne of God, because He alone can judge the motives of men's hearts.

The Word of God clearly warns us, "So be careful not to jump to conclusions before the Lord returns as to whether someone is a good servant or not. When the Lord comes, he will turn on the light so that everyone can see exactly what each one of us is really like, deep down in our hearts. Then everyone will know why we have been doing the Lord's work. At that time God will give to each one whatever praise is coming to him" (1 Corinthians 4:5, TLB).

Remember, by the judgment you give, you will be judged also.

Chapter 26

Touching Heaven "Alone"

Unless we are praying and spending time alone with God, we really can't understand what it means to follow Christ. We are deceived by thinking that dynamic preaching, a good worship service, special music, great choruses, and an outstanding church program are where it's all at. But they're not.

We see in the Bible that one of the strongest agendas God has is to get people all alone. For example, Jacob ran 20 years or more. Finally, when God got him alone, He could make him into Israel.

You see, when it is only God and you, you are more apt to face your pride and your sins. With everyone else we argue these things away and look wonderful and smile. But when we are all alone before God, we face ourselves, and the cleansing and purification will take place.

We become less phony the more we are with the Lord. I cannot tell you strongly enough that each of us must develop a very strong habit of prayer; otherwise, our Christian walk will greatly lack reality.

But this is only the first step in God's agenda for each of

our lives. The next step is for Him to show us the desperate faces of 3.8 billion[1] people who are unreached with the Gospel. Each of them is created in the image of God with a soul that lives forever. Yet they are bound in the chains of sin and heading toward hell without knowing there is a name to call upon for salvation. God searches for those people who will stand in the gap on their behalf and intercede for their souls.

I am not talking about a little phrase we say at the dinner table: "Lord, please bless our food and our family, and save the poor heathens in Africa." I am talking about entering into incredible spiritual warfare. This means going consciously into battle against the powers of darkness for the release and freedom of people who cannot help themselves and don't have anyone else to fight for their deliverance.

It is basically the hardest, most agonizing, and difficult job we can ever embrace—but the only one that guarantees absolute victory.

It is amazing how easily we can get people in the Body of Christ motivated to demonstrate, to wear T-shirts, to collect signatures, or to raise money for a worthy cause. But it is the hardest thing to get them to pray for a world that is lost without Christ.

Why are our views and priorities so distorted? Why are we so easily distracted from the one thing that really would get the job done? The answer is because we are up against an enemy who knows what can hurt him the most! The devil is well aware that prayer is our most powerful weapon—it defeats him every time. With it, we touch heaven and cause the hand of God to move in a mighty way. Therefore, the devil would rather see us doing every other Christian activity instead.

At Gospel for Asia, both on the mission field and in the home office, we consistently experience that prayer is the quickest shortcut to victory. What would take us 50 years of struggles to accomplish, God can do in no time at all.

But how can you start, and what can you pray for? Just watch the news on TV or read the international page of a newspaper. Scribble on a piece of paper what is happening in Myanmar, Afghanistan, China, and other nations. Start praying for the needs of these nations. Put up a world map in your house and get the book called *Operation World* by Patrick Johnstone, which gives you a lot of information on the spiritual conditions of each country. Take Gospel for Asia's SEND!™ newsmagazine and other mission publications; go through them and make every article a matter of your intercession. Soon you will discover that 30 minutes, one hour, or two hours will not be enough to even scratch the surface.

It is the incredible wisdom of our God to ordain prayer to be the most powerful weapon of the church. If He had chosen anything else—like preaching, singing, money, or education—many of us could never participate in fighting the war.

But prayer doesn't require any talent and can be done anywhere, anytime, and by anyone. A housewife, a poor person, a child, a 90-year-old grandmother, an executive, or a lonely believer in a nursing home all are able to change the world and help change the destiny of millions of people through prayer.

If the Lord has spoken to you today, please respond by doing just one thing: "Pray!"

Chapter 27

It Can Be Done

A few months ago, when my family was with me in India and Nepal, my wife and a couple from our Indian office staff took a two-day train ride to another state.

When my wife came back, she shared with me about her trip. She said, "While we were traveling in the train, I was sitting up late in the evening looking out of the window into the dark night. As the countryside was flying by, I could see tiny lights coming from thousands of little huts scattered everywhere. In my heart I began to wonder how we would ever be able to reach all those people with the Gospel."

I told my wife, "It is true that India is a huge country with an enormous population. We must reach them one person at a time and one village at a time."

Our confidence and encouragement are this: God will never ask anything from us that cannot be done! If there is a thought of impossibility, it is always with us—never with Him. He has solutions and ways prepared in His infinite wisdom about which we would never even dream. Isaiah 55:9 says, "For as the heavens are higher than the earth, so are My ways higher than your ways, and My thoughts than your thoughts."

For example, who could have ever imagined that when Moses led the Israelites out of Egypt, God's plan was to part the Red Sea as they were being pursued by Pharaoh's army with no evident way out? Or who else other than this wonderful God could give His servant Joshua the confidence to pray for the sun and moon to stand still until the battle was won?

We serve this same God today. His thoughts and ways are still higher than ours. He already has answers and solutions about how to reach these billions of people with the Gospel. We can be confident that His ideas are much better and more effective than any of ours.

But how can we know the mind of God? The answer is by walking so closely in obedience to Him each day that He can guide and direct every single step we take.

Jesus is our example. The Son of God became the Son of man and demonstrated for us what it means to live a life that brings glory to the Father.

Jesus was not motivated by the desperate needs around Him. In fact, when He heard that Lazarus, the one He loved dearly, was sick, He could have easily gone and instantly healed him. But instead, He simply said that His time was not yet come. True, it was the Father's will for Lazarus to be raised up. But according to the Father's plan, it was not yet time. So Jesus waited for several more days for the exact moment to come. Jesus never acted out of urgency but out of His obedience to His Father's plan and purpose.

Jesus told us that just as the Father sent Him, He is also sending us. First Peter 2:21 says that we are called to follow in His footsteps.

Even so, much of Christian activity today is done in the energy of the flesh. The day of judgment will prove that it was nothing but wood, hay, and stubble. All will be turned into just a pinch of ash. God will make sure that no product of the flesh will remain in eternity, even things that were done in the name of the Lord.

After three and a half years of teaching His disciples, the

Master finally summed up all He had tried to teach and demonstrate to them—that without Him they could do nothing (John 15:5). Jesus said, "You are the salt of the earth" (Matthew 5:13). How much salt does it take to flavor food? Not much at all. But if the salt is without its saltiness, you can pour a mountain of it on your meal, and it will be useless. You see, the saltiness in us is the life of the Lord that flows through us unhindered. The mountain of activity that is done with our genius inventions, budgets, schemes, and plans all means nothing because His very life is missing. It is all contaminated with our soulish strength and carnal reasoning. It is useless.

In the first century, a handful of people made a huge impact on their society because the life of the Lord flowed through them—when one community saw them, they simply cried out, "These who have turned the world upside down have come here too" (Acts 17:6).

Turning our world upside down—world evangelism and proclaiming the Lord's kingdom in our generation—will never become a reality if we depend on the thousands of conferences, organizations, schemes, and plans developed with specialized computer programs and Madison Avenue techniques. God is still looking for a minority of people who will seek His face with all their heart and do the work in His strength.

In one of his children's books, C. S. Lewis describes a land cursed by a witch to have an endless winter. It is a difficult, cold time for all the creatures who live there. There is much suffering and hopelessness. But one day everything changes. A thaw begins. The birds, animals, and flowers appear everywhere. Life bursts forth once more because Aslan—the great Lion, the Son of the great Emperor over the sea—is coming. It is His land, and He comes to set it free. The creatures are heard saying, "Aslan is on the move." And then they sing: "When He shakes His mane, we shall have spring again."[1] The whole scene changes as the Lion advances into the cold, wintry land, and the power of the witch is finally broken.

This is what Jesus does. We can strive with all our own strength, energies, and resources to do His work and reach this generation with the Gospel, but in the end it will all be for nothing. The little that we can do will be a total waste because it will have been produced in the energy of the flesh. If, on the other hand, we can come to the place of total submission to His Lordship—doing what He wants us to do in the way He wants us to do it—then we will have accomplished the task. God told Jeremiah: "Call to Me, and I will answer you, and show you great and mighty things, which you do not know" (Jeremiah 33:3). I believe this challenge is meant for us as well. God wants to share His thoughts and plans with us for winning these nations for Jesus, but He expects us to ask Him how.

We will have confidence in the Lord's strength as we face seemingly overwhelming or impossible goals set before us, because we will have His thoughts and not our own. And the fruit of our labors will not only be effective but eternal.

A man or woman who knows God intimately will never be intimidated or controlled by anyone or anything.

Chapter 28

Fighting the Law of Attrition

Nothing stays the same! Just one look at your car will confirm this. The tire tread is wearing thin, the muffler is rusting out, and the engine will only go so many miles. Our houses have the same tendency. The paint peels off, the roof leaks after a few storms, and the tile and carpet don't seem to stay clean for more than a couple of days. In the kitchen the milk goes sour, the bread molds, and the peach that looked so delicious three days ago starts to rot.

Even things we leave completely alone, like the pictures on the wall or the books on the shelf, collect dust, change color, and become old. Half our time is spent washing clothes, cleaning house, and repairing things that break down. We do this because we know that, unless we continually work on maintaining our possessions, we surely will lose them to deterioration.

Exactly the same is true for our spiritual lives. Check it out for yourself by comparing your life and your ambitions with the ones you had when you first understood that Jesus wanted to use you to help win millions of people for His kingdom.

As time has gone by, your once-tender heart is now unmoved by the truth that, today alone, 80,000 souls will plunge into hell because they have died without calling upon the name of Jesus. Your eyes no longer have tears as you look at your world map and see the Muslim nations that are closed to the Gospel. You used to consider it a joy to write a check to support a native missionary, enabling him to reach his own people for Jesus. Today you're almost sorry that you made that commitment because you would rather spend that money on yourself, like buying the newest CD from your favorite Christian music group.

You remember when you couldn't wait to attend the prayer meeting for missions or to spend an hour alone in intercession for the lost world. Now you find it difficult to fit the prayer meeting in your busy schedule, and you have to kick yourself to get out of bed for a five-minute prayer.

Believe me, this is the situation for all of us: if our commitment and our call to serve God are left unattended. They will slowly deteriorate and be replaced with excuses and a thousand other things to do. We will then argue for our rights, our freedom, and justify our lack of time and interest in the cause. Finally, our other involvements will become more important than the call of God on our lives.

Let me ask you, what caused a man like Adoniram Judson, America's first foreign missionary, to be so different from us in his level of commitment and the achievement of his goal? What gave him the strength to go through incredible persecution and suffering, burying his first wife and three of their children on the mission field of Burma? Is it because he was a product of a different culture than ours in which the people and circumstances were more stable?

No, I don't believe so. Each person has his own struggles and problems. I firmly believe Judson was able to bear even the greatest of losses and pay the highest of prices because he had made a lifetime commitment to win the Burmese to

Christ or to die trying.

He deliberately kept his focus on his call and purpose, rejecting everything that would distract him from reaching his goal. God saw his heart and gave him the necessary grace to finish the race.

Another model of focused commitment is the life of George Whitefield.

> George Whitefield, the great British evangelist, was often falsely accused and maligned. The clergy spoke out against him, artists painted mocking portraits of his meetings, and slanderous tracts were published to attack him. But when his friends urged him to defend himself against the lies he refused. "I am content to wait till the judgment day," he said, "for the clearing up of my character. When I am dead I desire no epitaph but this, 'here lies G. W. What kind of man he was the great day will discover.'" He had committed himself to the Lord. He was looking beyond this world.
>
> Though [Whitefield] wrote Journals of his ministry during its first three years, he thereafter refused to take any steps towards making a correct knowledge of his life available. With his eye fixed on his accounting in heaven, he sought no justification of himself on earth" (Arnold Dallimore). What a contrast with the hypocrites who justified themselves in the sight of men—but God knew their hearts (Luke 16:15). And He knows our hearts too.[1]

Our greatest problem is that we continually lose our focus. We allow ourselves to be sidetracked by the world, by our mixed-up motives, and by our lack of discipline. It takes a radical commitment to live for the one goal God has set before us—to win the lost. Whatever part you have in it—be it to go, to intercede, to give, to send—make it the focus of your life. Start measuring everything that comes your way by this question: will it further the cause God called me to, or will it be an extra weight and additional distraction in running the race? Learn to walk away from things and even people who will take up your time, your emotions, and your money and thus hinder you from fulfilling God's purpose for your life.

Like Judson and Whitefield, we must continually work on keeping our focus to be able to run our race with endurance—and win it.

Wearing out the saints (Daniel 7:25) slowly is the master tactic of the enemy. Don't let him!

Chapter 29

The Small Pond and the Big Picture

The fishing boat was turning to shore after a night of fishing when a kingfisher swooped down and snatched a tiny fish out of the water. Suddenly, the bird lost its grip, and the small fish fell into a pond. Half dead, it struggled back to life. Meanwhile, a large fish approached and said, "What are you doing in my kingdom?" The large fish boasted that he was king over the only kingdom where fish live.

Hearing this, the little fish replied, "If only you could see where I'm from." And the little fish tried to explain about the vastness of the ocean, all the different kinds of fish, the ships, and the whales. The larger fish looked at him in disbelief. And the little fish said, "Well, how would you know? You've never left this tiny pond."

This story humorously illustrates how we become so used to "our" tiny corner of the world that we easily forget the big picture. As soldiers enlisted in the army of Jesus Christ, we, too, tend to think that our little battle is the only one going on, when in reality it's just a very small fraction of the global war we are called to fight.

Take a look at the life of the apostle Paul. Here is a man

who wouldn't take no for an answer, regardless of the opposition. He endured imprisonment, beatings, shipwrecks, starvation, loneliness, abandonment, and a host of other problems, yet he went forward with one thing on his mind—to preach the Gospel to those who had never heard.

How did Paul and the other apostles survive without giving up hope? They did not allow themselves to get caught up in their own struggles, and they never lost sight of the big picture. In Romans 8:18 Paul says, "For I consider that the sufferings of this present time are not worthy to be compared with the glory which shall be revealed in us."

While overseas last month, I experienced discouragement. When taping my broadcasts, I sometimes start at 3:30 a.m. One morning when the alarm went off, I didn't want to get up. I began to complain, "Why me? This is not fair. I went to bed late, and now after only two hours of sleep I must get up."

Then I sat up and spoke out loud. "I am in a battle. What I do today will touch the lives of millions. Lord, you promised that those who wait on you will renew their strength. Lord, I wait on you, and I know my strength will be renewed." Ten to 15 minutes went by with me praying and saying God's Word out loud. By the time I was ready to get back to the studio, I was a brand-new person with excitement, peace, and His strength.

What made the difference? I took my eyes off my own struggle and saw the big picture. I saw in my mind the battle that rages all around the world with this generation being enticed by the powers of darkness, bound by Satan's chains and moving hopelessly toward eternity. I saw a picture of a mighty army filled with the Holy Spirit moving all over the world preaching the Gospel and calling millions to repentance, and I saw those millions responding and giving their lives to Jesus.

When the enemy attacks us as we are serving the Lord, we

must remember that there is more going on than what we see around us. We must interpret our little pond, our little world, in light of the much bigger world.

I will never forget what Narayan Sharma, Gospel for Asia's leader in Nepal, said, "Sometimes it's so unbearably hot. Sometimes it's so cold that you don't want to move; but by any means, it is good to serve the Lord." This man lives with the reality of the big picture.

In your life you will face days in which you won't want to pray. Your emotions will be dry. This is the time when you need to stand up by faith and say, "I hang on to God's Word and will not drown in my own small pond." Perhaps you will be tempted to stop supporting your native missionary. But look at the big picture! That one native missionary you pray for and support will touch many villages, and hundreds of thousands will come to know the Lord Jesus Christ. Someday you will stand with that multitude rejoicing around the throne.

Are you discouraged? Do you want to give up? Are you having a difficult time looking beyond your own little world? If so, stick close to Jesus. Look into His eyes and receive His strength. Don't let the devil keep you intimidated, discouraged, and focused only on your own little world. God's kingdom is bigger! Let us rise up and shake off the deception of the enemy. Like Paul, let us never lose sight of the big picture, and let us gladly give our lives so that others may come to know Jesus.

One look at yourself and 10 looks at Jesus will keep you going.

Chapter 30

The Greatest Motivator of All

It's amazing how many Christian activities average believers participate in at one time or another during their Christian life. They feed the hungry, sing in the choir, teach Sunday school, collect clothing for the homeless, visit prison inmates, witness on the streets, volunteer in a nursing home, demonstrate for a moral issue, collect money for sick children, support a missionary, help the elderly, and so on.

Surely all of these good causes are a help and blessing to others. However, often I have wondered what the true motivation is behind an individual's involvement in the kingdom of God. For some it is the challenge and excitement of being involved in something significant. For others it is the need for fellowship and love. Some like the honor and glamour that come with the action. Others are motivated by guilt because they have so much more than those poor people on the street or in prison. Then, of course, there are always those who hope that their faithful service will ensure them a sizeable reward in heaven. Last, there are those believers whose hearts are truly burdened and touched by the suffering of others and the needs of a lost and dying world.

However, when we look in the Bible, we find that none of those motivations is good enough to get us through the hard times ahead, which Paul describes so clearly in 2 Timothy 3:1-4. They are insufficient to keep us committed until the end.

Jesus was filled with compassion when He saw the widow whose son had died, and when He encountered the sick, the blind, the demon possessed, and the multitude who were lost like sheep without a shepherd. But when it came to Jesus dying on the cross for our sins, it wasn't just compassion that motivated Him. It was His love for His Father in heaven! Out of this love relationship came the motivation to be obedient unto death and to say "Lord, I came to do thy will" and "Not my will be done, but thine."

You see, our commitments are so short-lived and we change from one worthy cause to another; because, as soon as difficulties and disappointments come our way, our motivation is also gone. Furthermore, excitement, honor, and compassion will not carry us very far, but love will.

Remember Jacob, who served Laban for 14 years in order to receive Rachel's hand in marriage? It was an enormous price of service he had to pay. Yet amazingly the Bible says that it seemed to him like just a few days because he loved her (Genesis 29:20).

The apostle Paul wrote at the end of his life to Timothy, "I have finished the race, I have kept the faith" (2 Timothy 4:7). What was the motivation behind such a life? It was this: "the love of Christ compels us" (2 Corinthians 5:14).

Hudson Taylor, the great missionary to China, was working hard for many years and struggling to keep his commitment until he discovered "the exchanged life," which means to be motivated by love for the Lord rather than by duty. A. B. Simpson, founder of the Christian Missionary Alliance, tells us how he learned this lesson

in his own life. As a young pastor, he struggled to serve
the Lord in his own strength, until he was broken down
in health. Finally, he met with God in such a way that it
changed his whole outlook on ministry. He expressed his
experience in these powerful words:

> "Once it was the blessing, now it is the Lord;
> Once it was the feeling, now it is His Word;
> Once His gift I wanted, now the Giver own;
> Once I sought for healing, now Himself alone.
>
> Once 'twas painful trying, now 'tis perfect trust;
> Once a half salvation, now the uttermost;
> Once 'twas ceaseless holding, now He holds me
> fast;
> Once 'twas constant drifting, now my anchor's
> cast.
>
> Once 'twas busy planning, now 'tis trustful
>   prayer;
> Once 'twas anxious caring, now He has the care;
> Once 'twas what I wanted, now what Jesus says;
> Once 'twas constant asking, now 'tis ceaseless
> praise.
>
> Once it was my working, His it hence shall be;
> Once I tried to use Him, now He uses me;
> Once the power I wanted, now the Mighty One;
> Once for self I labored, now for Him alone.
>
> Once I hoped in Jesus, now I know He's mine;
> Once my lamps were dying, now they brightly
> shine;
> Once for death I waited, now His coming hail;
> And my hopes are anchored safe within the veil.

All in all forever, Jesus, will I sing,
Everything in Jesus, and Jesus everything."[1]

Once I met a young native missionary in Rajasthan, India, during a workers' conference. His name is Par. When he first came to his pioneer field, he encountered severe opposition. Several of his enemies held him up in the air by his legs and told him, "We will tear you in half if you ever come back!"

But Par went back and preached in the streets, witnessed to people, and passed out Gospel tracts. Wasn't he afraid? Did he not take the warning seriously? Oh yes, he was afraid, and he knew his enemies meant what they said. So what gave him the strength and the motivation to risk his life? It was his love for Jesus, nothing else.

Today there is a church in this village with 104 believers.

Love is the greatest motivator of all. John 3:16 tells us, "God so loved the world that He gave His only begotten Son." He gave Jesus not out of compassion or pity, but out of love.

We, too, will have the strength to follow the cross and be faithful unto death if our motivation is love. One of the tests that reveals our heart's condition is to ask ourselves, "Why am I doing this or saying this? Is it for something I can get out of it, even a 'thanks' from others, or simply because I love Him?

Love Him more than life itself, for He is your life.

Chapter 31

"I Will Not Come Down!"

Two students flung from a speeding train in Gujarat . . . our Nepali leader arrested and standing trial for preaching the Gospel . . . one native missionary stabbed to death and another critically wounded in Nagaland . . . our Tamil language broadcaster dead as a result of a bus accident . . . a church burned to the ground in Karnataka . . . Bible school students and teachers attacked by a gang of angry Muslims in Andhra Pradesh . . .

These are just a few of many incidents Gospel for Asia experienced in a single 10 month period. Interestingly, these things happened almost simultaneously with tremendous victories and progress for the Gospel in previously unreached areas of the 10/40 Window. Is this just a coincidence, or is there more happening than we can see with our physical eyes?

The apostle Paul explains such happenings in Ephesians 6:12: "For we do not wrestle against flesh and blood, but against principalities, against powers, against the rulers of the darkness of this age, against spiritual hosts of wickedness in the heavenly places."

You see, we are engaged in spiritual warfare with none other than Satan himself and his demon forces, whose only goal is to stop any advancement of the Gospel of Jesus Christ. The Bible reveals to us that Satan has a highly organized system with which he controls and manipulates nations, world systems, and individuals for their destruction.

Unless we are fully conscious that we are engaged in spiritual warfare against the powers of darkness, we will not be able to accurately discern the attacks on our personal life and our ministry. Furthermore, our response to these events will be ineffective and powerless. The devil wants us to believe that we are not dealing with spiritual issues, and that we can solve our problems with human wisdom such as education, psychology, and philosophy. But these are big lies to keep us from using the weapons God has provided for us to destroy the attacks of the devil and to be victorious.

Paul tells us to "put on the whole armor of God" and then describes each of the weapons given to us: "having girded your waist with truth, having put on the breastplate of righteousness, and having shod your feet with the preparation of the gospel of peace; above all, taking the shield of faith with which you will be able to quench all the fiery darts of the wicked one" (Ephesians 6:11, 14-16).

The life of Nehemiah is a powerful illustration of how to engage in spiritual warfare dressed in the full armor of God. When God laid the need to rebuild the wall of Jerusalem on Nehemiah's heart, Nehemiah never compromised the truth of God's Word. We see a man who faced tremendous battles—physical hardship, deception, opposition, agony, misunderstanding, and discouragement. Many of Nehemiah's problems were caused by the very people he tried to help, yet he confronted his people with their sins and showed them a way to repent and live for God. He trusted the Lord for the impossible and overcame all the obstacles and enemy attacks through his faith in the God of Israel.

Nehemiah never allowed fear to sidetrack him from his goal. When a false prophet urged him to hide in the temple, Nehemiah immediately recognized him as an enemy agent. He knew he would sin against God if he allowed fear to enter his heart. Hebrews 11:6 says, "But without faith it is impossible to please Him." As soon as fear replaces faith,

God can no longer answer our prayers or fight on our behalf, because His promises will not work apart from faith.

Furthermore, Nehemiah never permitted any person or any circumstances to stop his work or slow him down. He consistently kept his focus in spite of threats, hardship, and offers of compromise. The only answer he had for those who tried to distract him or stop him was this: "I am doing a great work, so that I cannot come down" (Nehemiah 6:3). Without his immovable focus on the end result, the wall never would have been completed.

Finally, in the face of increased enemy attacks, Nehemiah's response was never to retreat. Instead, he had his men fully armed and ready for battle at all times: "with one hand they worked at construction, and with the other held a weapon" (Nehemiah 4:17).

But Nehemiah was not insensitive to the fears and worries of his people, especially after the wall was joined together and their enemies conspired to wipe them all out. He knew what to do in such a dangerous situation: "Nevertheless we made our prayer to our God" (Nehemiah 4:9). We, too, have no other alternative than to come to the Lord in prayer, asking Him to defeat for us the powers of darkness that seek to destroy us and the work of God.

Nehemiah and his people experienced God's presence in the midst of their trials and won a tremendous victory in the end. As we live for Jesus and fight the battle to advance His kingdom, we, too, will encounter the same opposition Nehemiah faced from the enemy. Let us determine to wear the full armor of God and carry the weapons of our warfare at all times. Only then will we be able to defend ourselves and win the battle through God's grace.

Rise up and shake off anything that's holding you down. You are a follower of Christ, a soldier enlisted by the Master Himself for His kingdom. You have been given all authority by your Lord. Be what He called you to be—an overcomer.

Don't forget that you are in a battle.

Chapter 32

Walking in His Shoes

When I first came to the United States, I visited a large, well-known church where the pastor announced an evening prayer meeting. I came early that night, genuinely concerned that I might not find a place in the sanctuary. I waited and waited for the thousands of believers I had seen in the morning to come and intercede for the pastor, the church, and the mission field; but in the end only seven showed up. It was an experience I will never forget, because on the mission field in India I had learned that, as a follower of Christ, prayer was the most important factor in life.

When you and I truly understand Jesus' love for the lost world, then we will sometimes feel like Elijah did: left all alone with our concern for the unreached. We call out and urge believers to invest their lives so that people groups living in the 10/40 Window can hear the Gospel, but our voices are so often drowned out by all the other activities going on in the Christian realm.

Most of these activities are designed to make life on earth more enjoyable and comfortable. That's what believers have come to expect, and that's the reason very few will show up for events like prayer meetings. Sacrifice, suffering, and intercession for the lost world are largely unpopular in many of our churches because they involve hard work and giving up comfort, time, and money.

When we look at the world situation, however, we can hear Jesus say loud and clear in His Word: "As the Father has sent Me, I also send you" (John 20:21). Jesus is asking us to be in His place, to walk in His shoes, and to become deeply concerned about the lost in our generation in countries like Albania, India and Mongolia.

There are people—thank God—whom He is calling to stand in the gap and who are willing to pay the price. If you have answered His call, don't get discouraged, feeling that the job is so huge and that only a handful of people share your burden. Remember, Jesus had only 12 disciples, yet they impacted their entire generation.

We must never lose the freshness of the privilege the Lord has given us—out of millions of people—to share His heart and be concerned about the lost world. We are given the opportunity to pray, to give, to go, to send missionaries and to make a huge difference for millions of people for all eternity. As we intercede for the unreached, we must allow God's love and compassion to fill our hearts. Our prayers will be so much more fervent and real if we identify with the people for whom we pray. That's what Daniel, Jeremiah, and Nehemiah did, and God answered them in a powerful way.

As you read news reports about events like the cyclone that hit the coast of Andhra Pradesh, put yourself in the place of that mother whose child was swept away by the tidal wave, or that man who found his wife and children dead under the rubble of their collapsed home. You will feel their pain, desperation, and hopelessness at not knowing the name of Jesus.

Pray for the people and events you read about in the newspaper or hear about over the radio and TV as if it were your own life. When you intercede for the unreached, don't let your prayers be in neutral. Like a gearshift in a car, let us shift into active faith and watch God give us whole nations! All things are possible for those who believe.

One day thousands from the heathen lands will stand before the throne of God worshiping the Lamb. We will meet them and rejoice with them. That moment will be worth all our prayers and sacrifice on their behalf.

Jot down prayer points from the news you hear and start praying for the world today.

Chapter 33

Dangerous Ground

Some time ago I found a colorful church flier in my mailbox. It was an open letter from the pastor of a large congregation. He invited the whole community to attend a series of high-class, Christian concerts he had lined up at his church. In his letter he wrote, "Ever since I first came to this church, it has been my highest priority to offer the finest and best Christian entertainment to the people of [this city]."

This pastor is definitely not alone in his pursuit to draw and impress crowds with his outstanding programs. Other churches do the same with their advertisements of the largest auditorium in town, the best interior decoration and comforts, the most spectacular Christmas pageant, the biggest budget, the newest sound equipment, or the largest church membership.

Two things are strangely absent in all this competition for numbers, glamour and success: the cross and the lost world! Once they were the center of the Gospel message; but for so many congregations and believers, there is very little room left in their lives or thoughts for these most vital conditions of discipleship.

Because they are no longer popular, they have been replaced with all sorts of self-centered activities. Quantity, size, and success impress us, but they do not impress God. This is evident even in creation. The earth, compared to the other planets, is so tiny and insignificant. Yet this is where God chose to carry out His eternal plans.

From the beginning of time, God's greatest concern has been to have a pure testimony to His name. This means His Word, His goals, and His priorities cannot be changed by any man. It also means that whoever is called by His name must live by His terms and preserve the purity of His Gospel.

We tread on very dangerous ground if we don't preach and teach the cross in fear that our membership will decrease. The same is true if we don't speak up when our church spends millions of dollars on an elaborate auditorium but has no burden, no prayer, and no money for the more than 3.8 billion[1] people who sit in darkness—on their way to hell—having never been reached by the Gospel.

A. W. Tozer wrote: "Why do we build our churches upon human flesh? . . . For we teach men not to die with Christ but to live in the strength of their dying manhood. . . . But if I see aright, the cross of popular evangelicalism is not the cross of the New Testament. It is, rather, a new bright ornament upon the bosom of a self-assured and carnal Christianity. . . . The old cross slew men; the new cross entertains them. The old cross condemned; the new cross amuses. The old cross destroyed confidence in the flesh; the new cross encourages it."[2]

In the Old Testament, God wiped out multitudes and once even the whole world population (except Noah and his family) in order to preserve a pure testimony. What would happen to us and to our churches if God dealt with us in the same way, judging our compromises with instant death?

Even if everything we do looks so successful right now, eventually it will have to pass the test of purity described in 1 Corinthians 3:13 when we get to heaven. What a shock it will be to watch our lives' work and all our church programs go up in flames.

Today we stand at the crossroads and have a choice to make: do we choose the purity of the Gospel with the cross at the center and the Great Commission as our No.1 task, or do we continue to fool ourselves with a gospel that has little to do with the New Testament? The pure Gospel says,

• "If anyone desires to come after Me, let him deny himself, and take up his cross daily, and follow Me" (Luke 9:23).

• "If any one comes to Me and does not hate his father and mother, wife and children, brothers and sisters, yes, and his own life also, he cannot be My disciple. And whoever does not bear his cross and come after Me cannot be My disciple" (Luke 14:26-27).

• "As the Father has sent Me, I also send you" (John 20:21).

What is your answer?

Chapter 34

Selfishness

Here is an excerpt from a letter I recently received from the mission field.

Many times we were stoned while preaching, forced to leave the place where we ministered and the village we lived in, threatened not to win souls, denied a place to sleep or food to eat, commanded and forced by the army to public labor such as building railroad tracks. High inflation, sickness, lack of transportation, and the hot climate are constant hardships we face on our mission field. But we are assured by the Holy Spirit that the more we suffer for Him, the more rewards will be arranged for us in heaven.

"Three of my co-workers lost their lives within this last year and a half while serving the Lord in the villages. Among them was Brother Kwang Wa, one of our most effective workers. Though they are now gone to be with the Lord, the seed they have sown will bring forth plenty of good fruit: souls for His kingdom.

It almost sounds like an excerpt from a letter written by the apostle Paul 2,000 years ago, doesn't it? But this one just came from Gospel for Asia's leader on the Gangaw mission field in Myanmar. During the preceding few years, our brothers there had been able to establish 25 churches with 345 baptized believers, mostly from strong Buddhist and Animist backgrounds.

How was this possible in the midst of all the hardship, suffering, and death? We can easily detect the answer in their letter: they simply understood what it means to follow Christ and put the souls of others ahead of their own desires, safety, and comfort. They had no resistance to paying the price it took to win these people to Jesus.

I am constantly shocked when I travel to Western churches and discover how little people know about the most basic call of Christ: to lay down our own desires, pick up our cross, and follow Him. In the average church and through most Christian media, we are brainwashed with a selfish gospel. We are exhorted to first watch out for ourselves, our families, homes, health, security, and rights. Then, when all these things are well taken care of, perhaps we can consider others.

I strongly believe that the No. 1 enemy that keeps us from reaching the lost world is not the devil, but our self-centeredness.

Normal Christian life in the New Testament was always other-centered. Even when Paul was sitting in prison, he hardly talked about his own agony and suffering, but in all his letters he expressed much more concern for the churches, co-workers, and believers across Asia. The letter he wrote to Philemon is a wonderful example of this Christlike attitude. He poured out his heart on behalf of Onesimus, a runaway slave whom he had led to Christ. For Paul, prison seemed to be only incidental, not worthy to lament about or devote more than half a sentence to in his letter. He was serving His Lord and others, no matter where he was and regardless of his circumstances.

William Booth, the founder of the Salvation Army, lived by the same principle. When he was old and too sick to travel to a convention where 5,000 of his leaders and followers had gathered, he sent a telegram with his message to be read to the whole assembly. Everybody expected a special sermon because he was supposed to be their main speaker. However, when they opened the telegram, there was only one word on the page: "Others!"

It's so easy to fall into the trap of thinking that just because we live in an affluent nation and our children don't have to beg for food on the streets of Bombay, God must especially favor us. We must be so careful to avoid becoming self-centered; because if we live for ourselves, God will find no time or space in our lives in which we could think about the lost world and invest our lives for the salvation of others.

I have been walking with God and serving Him for more than 30 years, and still my greatest struggle is my selfishness. I do not want to pay the price often. You will have the same battle in your own set of circumstances. The grain of wheat just doesn't like to die! But I have found that following Christ is not a matter of whether we enjoy doing something, but rather a deliberate decision of consistent, constant obedience. That's where the victory is won and where the fruit will follow.

"Oh to be saved from myself, dear Lord, oh to be lost in Thee. It is no more I but Christ that lives in me." How easy it is for us to sing these words but so hard to live it. Are you choosing the way of the cross today? What about giving up some meals to fast and pray for the lost people groups in our generation? How about burning the wish list and "stuff" you plan to buy and spending that money for the preaching of the Gospel? What about giving your vacation time to go to the slums of Mexico City and minister for Jesus? More suggestions on how to live this radical life are mentioned in my book *Road to Reality*. Get a copy and read it. It will change your life.

It is time for us to die . . . but you must choose it.

Chapter 35

How Can I Make a Difference?

Did you realize that the Body of Christ lacks no funds to pay for the expenses of every one of God's ordained plans, including taking the Gospel to all nations?

"But Brother K. P.," you will immediately reply, "if this is true, what about all the desperate needs and heartbreaking stories we hear about the mission fields of Asia and other parts of the world?" The answer is simple: The money that God has entrusted to individual believers and local churches is tied up in properties, elaborate church buildings, houses, cars, boats, bank accounts, investments, fashion, entertainment, and self-serving programs.

Billy Graham once said, "The hardest thing for a man or a woman to do is to give their money. A person's money represents his time, his talents, his education, his sweat, his tears, his job, his toils; and when he converts them into currency and gives it, he is giving his life."

However, if we understood what our money does on the mission field, that is, what God is doing with it, we would be amazed and more than willing to sell even the clothes on our back to reach the lost world. The following story perfectly illustrates the eternal value of the money we give.

In northwest India a group of native missionaries was preaching the Gospel on the street. A man in his late 50s came and got a Gospel tract in his native language. This man was a Hindu Brahman landlord. He had cancer in his body; and in order not to bring shame to his family, he ran away from his home to commit suicide. Far away from his home now, he sat on the street corner and read about Jesus and how He died for him on the cross 2,000 years ago.

There was a prayer he could pray at the end of this tract for forgiveness of sins and peace. For the first time in this man's life, he not only read about Jesus, but he prayed to Him. He felt something happening to him—a peace began to fill his heart. He did not commit suicide that day, but instead he journeyed back home.

The next day he went to the hospital for the doctors to give him further checkups. To his amazement the doctors pronounced that he was completely cured. The doctors could give no explanation of how it happened. He told them he knew—the tract he read had cured him.

He traveled to the nearest mission station at the address on the Gospel tract and told our brothers what had happened to him. As they explained to him more about the Lord Jesus, he began to weep. Finally he said, "Now I know this Jesus is my God." Then he said to them, "I am the landlord in my village. Would you please come and make all my people Christians?" How innocent, how naive, and how little he knew about sharing the Gospel.

Two brothers went with him and began to preach the Gospel in this village. Dozens of people gave their lives to Christ and were publicly baptized. As they continued sharing, a strong church was developed in the community. The transformation of this village happened through one simple Gospel tract that cost less than what it costs to buy one pack of chewing gum.

Would the individual who gave that $1 or $10 have ever thought a few pennies of that money would be used to print a Gospel tract that in turn would touch the life of one individual, saving him, healing him, and as a result reaching a whole village with the Gospel? Probably not.

Consider the thousands of underground churches in mainland China. Most churches there are privileged if they have one or two Bibles for the entire congregation. Several years ago I was in China. I was totally amazed as I listened to the Chinese brothers explain the scarcity of Bibles. When I asked how they manage, they told me that they tear the Bible into sections and hand out 10 pages per family. Each family will copy down these pages and bring the portion back and then they are traded around so each family gets a different 10 pages.

What an incredible joy it will be for a person who stands before the throne of God to meet thousands of Chinese brothers and sisters whose church received Bibles through his faithful sacrificial giving. Can you imagine the joy, the thrill that will be?

Here's a third example: consider the 60 adults who came to the Lord Jesus Christ through hearing the radio broadcast in the northeast India state of Orissa. No missionary had ever gone into the community. The people had never seen a copy of the Bible or a Gospel tract. But now, in their native language, they heard the Gospel presented through the Gospel for Asia Athmeeya Yathra radio program. After weeks of listening to the program, the news began to spread from one individual to the next, and finally more than 60 people gave their lives to Christ. The families of these new believers were deeply impacted by the change that came into their lives. One of them wrote a letter to Gospel for Asia's office requesting "that book" our brother was talking and reading from. Soon we sent two missionaries to them. They were overjoyed when our missionaries came with the Bible and explained to them more about the Lord. The believers were baptized, and a glorious church was established.

That broadcast they heard, like nine others in different languages, was made possible through the support of an individual, family, or congregation that was willing to give its resources to reach the lost world by faith.

During World War II, Winston Churchill called Franklin Roosevelt over the telephone, and said, "Give the tools, and we will complete the job." Today that is exactly what tens of thousands of brothers and sisters scattered in the most unreached parts of our planet are crying out to us—to help them with our prayers and resources so they can complete the task.

We must take this request very seriously. I pray that we will ask ourselves the question, "What can I give or sell so I can give to reach the lost?" Selling out for Jesus is not a new doctrine. Read Acts chapter 2, and you will find that these people sold everything. They had one thing on their mind— to declare to the whole world that Jesus is alive.

I think about the man in Oklahoma City who called me one day weeping over the telephone. He had just finished reading my first book, *Revolution in World Missions*. He told me of his two expensive Mercedes Benz automobiles, his mansion, and all the other stuff he owned. He explained how brokenhearted he was when he realized that millions are lost without Jesus. Finally, he told me he had made a decision with his wife and children that they would sell these expensive cars and home and live modestly so they could spend the resources to preach the Gospel and to reach the lost.

1 John 3:16-17 says, "By this we know love, because He laid down His life for us. And we also ought to lay down our lives for the brethren. But whoever has this world's goods, and sees his brother in need, and shuts up his heart from him, how does the love of God abide in him?"

A day is soon coming in which we will stand before God to give an account for the way we squandered our resources on our own self-centered living. We are the prodigal church that squanders away the Father's wealth on the affair of an adulterous relationship with this present, passing world.

Your money today can be turned into eternal souls. Don't wait for someone to come and pester you for it, but look for ways to invest it as a good steward. Don't forget that soon all you have—everything—will be burned up (2 Peter 3:10). If you hold on to your resources tightly now, you will walk into eternity empty-handed—but with a lot of regret. On the other hand, if you give away what you have now to reach the lost souls, you will walk into eternity with an inheritance that will never perish. Jim Elliot aptly stated this irony: "He is no fool who gives what he cannot keep to gain that which he cannot lose."[1]

What will you do now? You must decide.

Chapter 36

You Must Choose

The meeting was over. It was one of the strongest messages I'd ever spoken on dying to self. Maybe that's why I was shocked when a lady came up afterward and asked me to pray for her problems with smoking and having a short temper. In talking to her, I learned she believed these were caused by demons! I told her, "What you need to understand is that you must deal with your flesh—not demons. You cannot cast out your flesh. You must crucify it."

Many today seek instant victory and spiritual depth through a crisis experience. They don't want to pay the price of discipline and putting their old nature to death. Even when seeking God, they still want to be in total control.

Jesus came to set us free from our self-centered, lukewarm nature and to change us into His own image (Romans 8:29). Our changed character is much more important than the experience, spiritual gifts, or miracles we often seek.

Let us take Jesus as our example. Romans 15:3 tells us that, "Even Christ did not please himself." He laid aside all His privileges as God and lived on earth as a normal human being. He totally depended on His Father for everything.

Furthermore, the apostle Paul told those around him to follow him as he followed Christ (1 Corinthians 11:1). How did Paul practice this in his life? "Like an athlete I punish my body, treating it roughly, training it to do what it should, not what it wants to" (1 Corinthians 9:27, TLB).

No one becomes godly without a deep commitment to a disciplined life. Dying to self is the door to godliness (Galatians 2:20). And it is a choice we must make.

Jonathan Edwards, the great American preacher and scholar, made 70 resolutions by which he patterned his daily life. He wrote this in his diary: "*Resolved*, never to lose one moment of time, but to improve it in the most profitable way I possibly can."[1]

Jesus asked us to choose to carry the cross. It is not imposed on us. Accepting inconveniences, fasting, praying, giving up our rights, living simply, seeking no honor or praise from men, giving sacrificially, being misunderstood, humbling ourselves, and avoiding self-centeredness—these are things we must choose.

Similarly, no one forced Jesus to do anything. He Himself chose the poverty, sleepless nights, hunger, thirst, rejection, loneliness . . . and finally, the cross. He exercised His freedom of choice to discipline everything in His life in order to obey His Father. As Hebrews 5:8 explains, "Though He was a Son, yet He learned obedience by the things which He suffered."

Paul's statement in Philippians 2:12, "work out your own salvation with fear and trembling," is taboo for many believers. God is not going to instantly make you holy— you must choose to obey so you can become holy. He will not make you godly without your commitment and work. For example, it took Moses 40 years to become Moses the deliverer. It took Joseph 13 years in prison to become prime minister of Egypt. It took years of discipline and commitment for Daniel to become someone who changed history. It took Jesus 30 years to preach the Sermon on the Mount.

Walk away from instant Christianity that offers no cross, hardship, or responsibility! It is false. Without consistent discipline in life, we will remain dependent baby Christians.

The following paragraphs[2] make up a list of practical disciplines compiled by a friend of mine to help develop a consistent, godly life. My prayer and hope is that this list of disciplines will become a blessing to you as it has been for me.

Begin with the simple things. A disciple will always seek to avoid making unnecessary work for others. So hang up your clothes. Make your bed promptly and neatly every morning. Clean up after yourself, and put your shoes in their proper place. Don't despise these small things as irrelevant to becoming spiritual. They are the very essence of it. They indicate that extra touch of foresight, carefulness, and thoughtfulness that makes the difference between a spiritual Christian and a carnal, lukewarm one.

Show respect to all—even to the poor and the lowly. When speaking or listening to someone, develop the habit of looking at him or her as if no one else mattered to you at that moment. When in a church meeting, discipline yourself to keep your eyes on the speaker instead of allowing your eyes to wander here and there. To gaze around at others or down at your feet is rude and discourteous, both to the Lord and to the speaker.

Tackle difficult tasks promptly. Do first the things that you would rather do last. Sit down right away and do the homework or write the letter (or article) that you have put off for so long. Welcome these difficult tasks. Cultivate a sense of responsibility in doing them faithfully. Ask yourself these questions:

• Can I be depended on to fulfill any task assigned to me?
• Am I quick to volunteer when a job needs to be done, or do I find myself slipping quietly away?
• Do I accept responsibility for my decisions . . . and for my mistakes as well?
• Can I be depended on in money matters?

Be punctual for meetings and appointments. The habit of being on time will never be acquired unless you are convinced that courtesy demands it and you plan ahead and allow yourself enough time to get to the appointed place. Don't allow yourself to waste time in idle daydreaming. Bring every thought into captivity to Christ. Make use of your spare time to read quality books, fellowship with someone, or help others.

When unexpected events throw your well-laid plans into confusion, don't let stress conquer you—for that is only foolishness. Instead, choose to believe that what seems to be nothing but human blundering is really the gentle steering of God for your very best (Romans 8:28). So give thanks to the Lord for His ordering of your life.

Keep your emotions under control. In conversations with the opposite sex, maintain a courteous reserve; this is because friendship can become affection, and affection can lead to lust—to the shock of both involved. That which began innocently may end disastrously. Don't let Satan make you say, "I couldn't help it." Pluck out the offending eye or cut off the offending hand or foot before it is too late. Your emotions may not immediately obey your will. But your actions must. In due course, your emotions also will follow the lead of your determined purpose and your decisive stand.

Master your moods. Discipline yourself to behave just as well when you "feel bad" as when you "feel good." Discipline yourself to read God's Word and do your work even when you "don't feel like it."

Discipline your tongue. Don't blurt out everything that comes to your mind. Frankness is a virtue only when it is coupled with intelligent, loving tact and discretion. Otherwise, it is evil and unnecessary.

Subordinate less important things to the more important ones. Select the things you must do, and do them first. If you "major in the minors" and allow your friends, impulses, and conveniences to dictate your priorities, you will end up as a mediocre Christian—useless to God and useless to men.

Submit graciously to God-given authority. Such discipline will round off your rough edges and also preserve you from much folly.

Control your curiosity. Don't be a busybody in others' matters.

Conquer gluttony. Eating is not a sin, but gluttony is. Paul said, " I will not be brought under the power of any. Foods for the stomach and the stomach for foods, but God will destroy both it and them. Now the body is . . . for the Lord" (1 Corinthians 6:12, 13). One should eat heartily and with enjoyment. But we should know what and how much is good for us, and have the self-control to stop when we should.

Learn to wait. To grab for something before God's time is to spoil it. There is a time in God's timetable for all things—in the matter of marriage, for example. Wait for that time, and don't rush ahead. Learn to respect the timetables that are found on life's joys, responsibilities, and privileges. We don't help God by opening a rosebud—we only spoil the blossom.

Systematic prayer and Bible reading are prime essentials for a disciplined life. The discipline of getting out of bed a few minutes early—at any cost—to spend time for this, every day, will itself bring rich rewards.

Avoid unnecessary luxuries and don't be wasteful in spending money. There are dangers in times of ease and prosperity that can be avoided only by some deliberate acts of self-denial on our part. Choose to miss a meal at times. "You therefore must endure hardship as a good soldier of Jesus Christ" (2 Timothy 2:3).

Our goal in life is Christlikeness, not a comfortable, self-serving, lukewarm life. Let us have a passion for improving the quality of our Christian life and fulfilling all of God's will. Let us be ready for sacrifice or for service, applying ourselves faithfully at all times to the task at hand.

Do all for Jesus sake!

Chapter 37

What Is It Worth to Me?

God's desire to conform us to the very image of His own Son sounds like a good plan to us and a worthwhile pursuit. We immediately think of all the wonderful things Jesus did while He was on earth, and we feel privileged that God wants to use our lives in a similar way.

Some of the things we admire the most in Jesus include His love for even the worst sinner, His faith to move mountains, His authority over demons, His power to heal, and His anointing to preach. We have no objections for God to conform us into such an image—until we find out that He is planning to accomplish this through breaking us . . . by means of the cross. His goal goes even beyond brokenness when it comes to our dearly loved "self" that sits on the throne of our lives.

If there is one Scripture in the entire Bible that speaks volumes of what it means to be filled with the Holy Spirit, to experience the fullness of the Lord, to have rivers of living water flow unhindered, and to be changed into His likeness, it is Galatians 2:20: "I have been crucified with Christ; it is no longer I who live, but Christ lives in me; and the life which I now live in the flesh I live by faith in the Son of

God, who loved me and gave Himself for me."

Think about this Scripture. The "I" that to each of us represents the most important person on earth, our own self, was nailed to the cross and died there. With it, the greatest obstacle for Christ's life to be seen through me is removed. Someone explained it like this: There is a cross and there is a throne in all of our lives. If "I" is on the throne, Christ is on the cross. However, if Christ is on the throne, then "I" is on the cross.

God knows that there is no peaceful co-existence possible between "self" and Christ. That's why He breaks me in so many areas of my life, until I willingly yield my "self" to death. Only in the measure in which I will allow this cross to operate in my life—to bring death to my own selfish ambitions, my ways, my rights, my reputation, and my interests—will I be able to allow Christ to manifest His life through me.

Jesus Himself never tried to walk away from either the process of brokenness or the cross because He knew very well that only through His death would we have life. There were times Jesus had the opportunity to save His own neck, but each time He made a deliberate decision to choose brokenness and death instead. For example, one of those times was when the Greeks came to Philip with the request: "Sir, we wish to see Jesus" (John 12:21).

The secular historian and contemporary of Jesus sheds a little more light on this story. In his writings he mentions that the king of a small kingdom sent several men to carry an urgent letter to Jesus. In this letter the king wrote a message that went something like this: Jesus, I have learned about You, and I understand that the Jews are plotting to kill You. I believe You are a good man and a good teacher. Why don't You come and be part of my kingdom and rule with me? We will take care of You. The historian continues his account by writing the reply that Jesus supposedly gave the king.

Interestingly, the answer is very similar to the one Jesus gave to those Greeks, recorded in John 12:23-26:

"The hour has come that the Son of Man should be glorified . . . Unless a grain of wheat falls into the ground and dies, it remains alone; but if it dies, it produces much grain. He who loves this life will lose it, and he who hates his life in this world will keep it for eternal life. If anyone serves Me, let him follow Me; and where I am, there my servant will be also."

Jesus was telling these Greeks, "If you really want to see Me, you must go where I go. My destination is the cross, where I will die in order to give life. If you truly want to see Me, you must choose the same road and die as well. Only through death will you find Me."

How hard you and I try, even in our Christian work, to preserve our own lives and avoid the pain that accompanies the process of brokenness and death to our dear selves! Jesus said that we indeed have the choice of saving our own lives and remaining just as we are. If this is our course of action, we can study the Bible for the next 15 years and become experts, but we still will not see Him.

In the Sermon on the Mount, Jesus taught that only the pure in heart will see God. That purity comes not only when my sins are forgiven, but when I no longer fight to preserve my life but allow God to take me through the same lifelong process of brokenness and death through which He led Jesus His Son.

You and I must answer this question: What is it worth to me to see Jesus?

Chapter 38

When We Have Failed—What Next?

When I was young, my friends and I would often run to the potter's house near our school. We little fellows would stand under the tall coconut tree in front of the potter's work shed and watch him and his wife make clay pots. Many times I saw the potter forming a beautiful vessel out of the lump of clay he had placed on his wheel. But all of a sudden, the pot would become marred, and the potter would take it off the wheel and throw it away.

Many people start out in their Christian life and in their service for God with wonderful dreams, incredible commitment, and great vision. No one around them can match the zeal and fire they have in their hearts. But somehow, whether through circumstances or by their own deliberate decision, knowingly or unknowingly, they make a wrong move—and everything in their life collapses. Regretting their loss, they sit in agony, wishing a thousand times that what they did had never happened. Often because of their failure, they feel that God has cast them aside, just like the potter discarded the marred clay pot.

Having been in ministry for over 30 years, I have confronted, counseled, talked with, and wept with many of God's people who made terrible mistakes in their lives. Some of them were servants of God who had been known for their strength, their uprightness, and the incredible ways God had used them. It was extremely painful for me to see them cut down by the enemy. I discovered that their despair over their failure was much deeper than what others felt because they realized the shame they brought on the name of the Lord and His church. Their struggle was not whether God would forgive their sin but believing that He still could, or even desired to, use them in His kingdom.

We Christians, who are supposed to be recognized by our love for one another, are very quick to judge, condemn, and write off completely those whose failures have become the talk of the town or the focus of the news media.

However, each time we write off one of our brothers or sisters who has failed so publicly, Jesus takes a long look into our hearts and says, "He who is without sin among you, let him be the first to throw a stone"(John 8:7, NASB). The truth is, we all have failed. The only difference is that our sin cannot be printed in the newspaper headlines because it's hidden in our hearts. We are so confident that we would never murder someone who offended us. But Jesus said that if we become angry with our brother—not just externally, but internally—we have already committed murder (Matthew 5:21-22).

The longer we walk with the Lord, the more we realize how far we are from God's standard. As He sheds His light in our hearts, we learn to see our lives with His eyes, and we recognize that even our so-called "small" failures are major hindrances to our spiritual growth.

One of my own struggles in life is with discouragement after God puts His magnifying glass on an area in which I'd thought I was doing so well. The failures He reveals to me have become a major reason for some of the darkest valleys

I've been through. Many times I've wept alone or cried myself to sleep over my sins and failures. By His grace, I have learned to return to the cross again and again to find strength to continue in the battle.

In light of God's perspective, even after 20 years of preaching, the great apostle Paul calls himself the chief of sinners (1 Timothy 1:15). The truth is, we all live with failure, no matter how old we are or where we are in life. The devil uses this fact as a powerful weapon to discourage us and keep us down. Because of past sin and failure, many of God's people live with an incredible amount of self-rejection, self-pity, guilt, condemnation, hopelessness, and remorse. They blame themselves or someone else and, as a result, lack the inner strength to go on. They can't find any answers to devastating questions like the following, which trouble their hearts:

•What can a woman say in her own defense when she is caught in adultery and brought before the court to be stoned to death? (John 8:3).

•How could this disciple ever repair the damage he did after he denied Christ—never even imagining this would happen? (Luke 22:61).

•What does a man do if his wonderful beginning ends with adultery and then murder to cover it up? Is there life after that? (2 Samuel 12:9).

•What happens when someone becomes physically sick because of sin? How could he ever find the courage to ask God to heal him, because he brought it on himself? (Psalm 32).

•How can a young man hope to ever make it in the ministry when his co-workers look down on him because he didn't perform well and the most famous apostle of all has labeled him as halfhearted? (Acts 15:38).

•How can a woman ever expect to stop hurting and be free of guilt and inner turmoil, having been through several marriages and divorces? (John 4:18)

Even if we cannot find any answers or solutions to our

marred and hopeless situations, the Bible has good news for us: God is in the business of making total failures into beautiful people. He does not rejoice over our failures—neither does He ignore them. But in His great mercy, He turns that which the devil meant for destruction into a stepping stone toward His purpose.

As a matter of fact, failure in our life is one of the most important tools God frequently uses to break, melt, and mold us so we can become more like Jesus on the inside.

Should there be any among us who think they are able, perfect, upright, and strong in themselves, they must know that God cannot use them to fight in His army in their own strength. Before picking up any of them, He must first lead them through deep valleys until they are broken and realize how helpless they actually are. That's what happened to Paul. With all of us, God will only begin on level zero, where we know by experience that without Him we can do nothing (John 15:5).

Yet for all those who have failed, the most painful questions of all remain: "What do I do when the vessel is marred and the original purpose is lost? Even if God should decide to give me a second chance, will He make something different and a little lesser out of my broken vessel than the original dream on His heart? Can I still fulfill God's perfect plan— the best He had for me—and not the second best? Where do I go from here? Is there a way out of this mess?"

Is it possible to recover, and recover fully? The answer is a thousand times "Yes!" . . . if only you can believe.

The Lord says, "For as the heavens are higher than the earth, so are My ways higher than your ways, and My thoughts than your thoughts"(Isaiah 55:9). Whenever it looks to us like the end, it's only the beginning for God. In God's workshop, the marred clay pot is not thrown away and forgotten. Rather, with great care, the Potter removes the impurity from the clay and later makes it into a better and more valuable vessel than before. You see, Jesus came to "give . . . beauty for ashes" (Isaiah 61:3).

To give us hope as well as instruction, the Bible is filled with illustrations of people who failed miserably. God worked with their failure, sin, and frailty and still was able to fulfill His perfect plan in their lives. Many of them became heroes of faith and examples for us to follow.

God's work began with creation. In Genesis 1:1-2, we read that the earth was formless, void, and full of darkness. God never created anything void, chaotic, or evil. It became that way through the fall of Lucifer. So what was God going to do with it—throw it away?

No, He began re-creating it with the words, "Let there be light." After each step, He paused and declared, "It is good—it's marvelous, wonderful, first-class!"

God re-created this planet that had been so filled with chaos and that had lost all its original beauty. He renewed it in such a way that it became the home for His Son's bride. It was definitely not a second-best place.

Adam and Eve were God's most precious creation. He took the clay in his own hands and, with great care, formed man in His own image (Genesis 1:27). The plans He had for their lives were incredible and wonderful. But the man and his wife failed miserably and had to be driven out of the Garden of Eden. An angel with a flaming sword was posted at the entrance to the garden so they would never be able to come back (Genesis 3:24). What was God going to do now after the whole purpose of man's creation—fellowship with Him—was lost?

He immediately gave them the most wonderful

prophesy in Genesis 3:15, the promise of the seed of the woman, who is the Lord Jesus Christ our Savior.

Does this mean the cross is God's second best because He lost his first plan for mankind when Adam fell? If we say that the Messiah and the cross (and what Jesus accomplished there through His death) are an inferior choice to God's original plan, it would be blasphemy! God's gift, "the Lamb slain from the foundation of the world" (Revelation 13:8), was God's greatest revelation of His love toward mankind, greater than what Adam ever experienced before his fall. And think about this: the original plan made man only in the image of God, whereas the second one made him a child of God (John 1:12). No, the cross is not the second best—it is the very best![1]

Moving through the book of Genesis, we encounter Abraham . . . what a mighty man of God! He was not only the father of the nation of Israel, but of Christianity as well. The Bible declares in Romans 4:16 that all those who believe are the children of Abraham. But this legacy began with lies and deception. Twice, to save his own neck, he put his wife's life and future in jeopardy by telling others she was only his sister. Then he had relations with a young woman—who was not his wife—and got her pregnant. All along, Abraham hoped God would be pleased with this detour and accept the child as the son of promise.

After all this, God picked Abraham up, used him, and even brought His own Son into the world through Abraham's line. When was the moment in Abraham's life in which God took this marred clay pot and remade it into the most beautiful vessel? It was when Abraham finally realized and admitted he was a hopeless case (Romans 4:19).

Then there was Jacob. Jacob is the classic example of a messed-up clay pot! Even before he was born, Jacob was chosen by God, as his parents were told, "The older shall serve the younger" (Genesis 25:23). What more could Jacob want? But he wasn't content to wait until God worked out the details of His promise. Jacob became a deceiver in order to get what was already his through God's plan. He had the audacity to pretend before his father and say, "I am Esau your firstborn" (Genesis 27:19).

As a result, Jacob wasted 20 precious years of his life. He became a nomad; lived in constant pain, agony, and turmoil; and missed out on every blessing he could have had in his home and with his family for all those years.

Finally, Jacob came to the end of the road. He wrestled with an angel, who asked him, "What is your name?" (Genesis 32:27). For the first time, he said, "[My name is] Jacob" (Genesis 32:27). With those words, he admitted that he was a deceiver and failure. And that's where his name was changed to Israel, meaning "prince with God."

In the Bible, it is interesting to note that God often introduces Himself like this: "I am the God of Abraham, Isaac and . . . Jacob." Why does God identify His almighty name with "Jacob," the deceiver who wasted 20 years of God's time, and not with the new name "Israel"?

The answer is this: through His name, His very identity, God wants to say to you and me, "I am still the God who makes failures into princes. I am still the God who picks up broken lives, failed marriages, people sick in body because of sin, those who've been in prison for 20 years, men and women labeled as losers, nobodies, and outcasts—and restores them beyond even their original beauty and purpose."

Another hero of the Old Testament is Moses, one of the greatest leaders who ever lived. According to God, he was the meekest, most humble man on the face of the earth (Numbers 12:3). But Moses didn't start out that way.

When God called Moses to do something, he was so naturally able that he ruined everything and became a murderer. For 40 years he had to live with that loss, left out and forgotten by the rest of the world. Finally, when God called him to deliver the nation of Israel, his answer went something like this: "God, I am a total failure. I can't even speak" (see Exodus 4:10). When God picked up Moses there in the desert of Midian, He remade this broken vessel into such beauty that God Himself declared, "There has not arisen in Israel a prophet like Moses" (Deuteronomy 34:10).

Then we read about Samson. What incredible physical strength Samson had! Yet he totally lacked moral convictions, and even common sense, when it came to women. Above all, Samson took the call of God on his life much too lightly. There came a day in Samson's life when he lost it all, when his vessel was not only broken but shattered into a thousand pieces as well. Then why do we find his name listed in Hebrews chapter 11? While forced to grind at the mill of his enemies—a prisoner, blind, and without hope—Samson must have surrendered his wasted life to the One who gives beauty for ashes. God testified that Samson accomplished more when he was blind and in his dying moments than when he was a free man and had his sight (Judges 16:30).

Reading on in the Old Testament, we read about Rahab, a prostitute, who used to stand every night at the street corner of the "red-light district" of Jericho, waving at potential customers. How did her name get into Matthew chapter 1? How was she chosen to be the great, great, great . . . grandmother of Jesus Christ? The only answer is that God's grace and ability to save, deliver, and make new are far beyond our comprehension.

Then there was Jonah. Jonah was a rebellious preacher up until the end of his Nineveh episode and perhaps even beyond. Why would the Son of God identify His name with Jonah's (Matthew 12:40)? The man had a real problem with deliberate disobedience and considered himself qualified to argue with Almighty God. In the end, Jonah got mad at God for accepting the repentance of the inhabitants of Nineveh and not striking them dead. God tried to teach him a lesson about mercy, but Jonah didn't get it. Finally, God quit talking to him on the subject, and the whole book of Jonah ends without any answer. We are not told what else transpired in his life, but surely God must have taken this disobedient vessel and turned Jonah into something so wonderful that Jesus could attach His name to him.

More examples abound in the New Testament. Peter, the apostle to whom Jesus gave the key to open the kingdom of the church to the Jews and to the Gentiles, never imagined that he would qualify for such a task after he had denied Jesus three times in a row. He must have thought that if anyone should be given this honor, it should have been John, the "beloved" disciple.

In fact, even after the resurrection, Peter didn't think he was good enough for any ministry at all. Deeply disappointed with himself, he said to the rest of the disciples, "I am going fishing" (John 21:3). However, even when Peter had given up on his usefulness to God, Jesus stepped in and in the most loving way restored him to the ministry and to a relationship with Him (John 21:15-19).

Thank God that one of Christ's disciples, the so-called "doubting Thomas," came to my village of Niranam, India, in A.D. 52. Would we have accepted him for missionary work with our organization? From all I read in the Gospels about Thomas, he would have never made it past the application form! But Jesus selected Thomas to go to one of the worst regions on earth to plant His church. What power and love the Lord has to transform someone so unqualified into a mighty apostle!

John Mark—what a blessing this man became to the whole church by writing the story of Jesus in the Gospel of Mark. He was the one who was rejected from Paul's ministry team because on his first assignment he deserted his teammates. In Paul's opinion, John Mark was a failure and didn't deserve a second chance (Acts 15:36-37).

How devastated and useless John Mark must have felt after the apostle Paul himself declared him unfit for his mission team. But God didn't give up on him. Rather, He used this failure to do a deep work in John Mark's life. The change must have been obvious, because even the apostle Paul was convinced that John Mark had become a different man and sent for him (2 Timothy 4:11).

There are so many others we could mention whose lives were marked by failure . . . and by God's grace, remaking them into the most beautiful vessels. Take time and read through Matthew chapter 1, and underline the names of all those who were total failures. You'll find prostitutes, crooks, those who committed incest, liars, murderers, and just about everything you can imagine—all that in Jesus' family, the line through which He chose to come.

The Bible tells us all these unedited life stories of God's heroes to give us this one message: when we have failed and all seems ruined, God is still able and willing to make the best out of our lives, not the second best. All He asks is that we repent, accept His forgiveness, and never look back. *When God forgives us it is as though the offense was never committed.*

In the lives of those who once were broken vessels, whom God picked up and in His mercy restored to beauty, we will find wonderful qualities such as real gratitude, a longing for holiness, deep humility, and compassion for others.

Please understand me correctly: we will *not* become better Christians in the end by sinning and failing as much as possible (Romans 3:8). Neither does God need or depend on our failures to work in our lives and teach us valuable lessons. If that were the case, He would not have been able to do any work in Jesus' earthly life because He never failed.

Even if we fail again and again, God is faithful to remake

our vessel each time. However, it is *not* part of His plan for us to take His grace lightly and carelessly continue to produce failures. He is expecting us to learn from our past mistakes, walk in humility, and honor Him with a life of obedience to His Word.

However, we must remember that as long as we live on this earth, the devil will try his best to trip us up. None of us should ever presume to have "arrived" and to be strong, experienced, and holy enough to never fail. Not even a spiritual rock who has been faithful for the past 50 years is immune to failure or the worst of disasters. The Bible warns us in 1 Corinthians 10:12: "Therefore let him who thinks he stands take heed lest he fall."

In the 18th century, Robert Robinson was saved under George Whitefield's preaching and became a wonderful man of God and a spiritual rock. He was the one who wrote this well-known hymn:

> Come, Thou Fount of ev'ry blessing,
> Tune my heart to sing Thy grace;
> Streams of mercy, never ceasing,
> Call for songs of loudest praise.[2]

Sadly, Robinson, who had blessed and encouraged so many with this song, wandered far away from those streams of life and the God who saved him. Like the prodigal son, he became involved in all the wickedness and worldliness of his society.

Years later, he was traveling by stagecoach and was sitting next to a young woman who, he noticed, was deeply fascinated by the book she was reading. When she came across a lyric she considered especially beautiful, she read it to Robinson and asked him what he thought of it. This is what she read:

> Prone to wander, Lord, I feel it,
> Prone to leave the God I love, . . .[2]

He broke out weeping, and with tears running down his face, he replied, "Madam, I am the poor unhappy man who wrote that hymn many years ago, and I would give a thousand worlds, if I had them, to enjoy the feelings I had then."

This encounter brought Robinson back into the outstretched arms of the living God. The Lord restored to him the long years that the cankerworm and the locusts had eaten (Joel 2:25).

God has a Father's heart, and each time we fail, He feels our pain and the agony we go through. Above all, He wants us to know that no matter how deep we fall or how badly our vessel is shattered, He is still greater! There is no failure in this world, no matter how severe and devastating it might be, that could prevent Him from fulfilling His perfect plan in our life—if we believe.

The overcomers are *not* the ones who have never failed but those who overcame by the blood of the Lamb (Revelation 12:11) that was shed for sinners and total failures.

It is time to get up and go home—Father is waiting for you (Luke 15:20-24).

Notes

Chapter 5

1. Paraphrased from a message taught by Zac Poonen at the Gospel for Asia Biblical Seminary in 1997.

2. From a tract by an unknown author.

Chapter 10

1. C. S. Lewis, *The Screwtape Letters*, New York, NY: Bantam Books, ©1982, p. 61.

2. Dietrich Bonhoeffer, *The Cost of Discipleship*, New York, New York: MacMillan Publishing, ©1963, p. 99.

3. SEND!™ September/October 1997 issue, Carrollton, Texas: Gospel for Asia, ©1997, p. 4.

Chapter 12

1. Michael L. Brown, *How Saved Are We?* Shippenburg, PA: Destiny Image, ©1990—Michael L. Brown, pp. 43-44.

Chapter 16

1. Global Evangelization Movement, 1998, www.gem-werc.org, population of "World A" plus "World B."

Chapter 18

1. Global Evangelization Movement, 1998, www.gem-werc.org, population of "World A" plus "World B."

Chapter 26

1. Global Evangelization Movement, 1998, www.gem-werc.org, population of "World A" plus "World B."

Chapter 27

1. C. S. Lewis, *The Lion, The Witch And The Wardrobe*, New York, NY: MacMillan Publishing, ©1970, pp. 64 and 75.

Chapter 28

1. Michael L. Brown, *How Saved Are We?*, Shippenburg, PA: Destiny Image, ©1990, p. 70.

Chapter 30

1. A.B. Simpson, a hymn entitled "Himself," *Hymns of the Christian Life*, Harrisburg, PA: Christian Publications, ©1978, p. 248.

Chapter 33

1. Global Evangelization Movement, 1998, www.gem-werc.org, population of "World A" plus "World B."

2. A.W. Tozer, *The Divine Conquest*, Old Tappan, New Jersey: Fleming H. Revell Company, ©1950, pp.57-60.

Chapter 35

1. Jim Elliot, *The Journals of Jim Elliot*, Old Tappan, New Jersey: Fleming H. Revell Company, ©1978, p. 174.

Chapter 36

1. Jonathan Edwards, quoted by Philip E. Howard, Jr., *The Life and Diary of David Brainerd*, Moody, 1949, p. 18.

2. Paraphrased from a tract, "How to Become a Disciplined Person," published in India.

Chapter 38

1. Taken from a message shared by Zac Poonen at the Gospel for Asia Biblical Seminary in 1997.

2. Robert Robinson, a hymn entitled "Come, Thou Fount," *Great Hymns of the Christian Faith*, Grand Rapids, MI: Singspiration, ©1966, p. 17.

Other Materials from Gospel for Asia

Books by K.P. Yohannan

The Coming Revolution in World Missions
In this exciting and fast-moving narrative, K.P. Yohannan shares how God brought him from his remote jungle village to become the founder of Gospel for Asia.

Suggested donation: $3 US/$3 CDN/£3 UK
Order Code: **B1**
On Audiocassette: $9 US/$12 CDN/£ UK
Order Code: **B1AC**

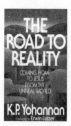

The Road to Reality
K.P. Yohannan gives an uncompromising call to live a life of simplicity to fulfill the Great Commission.

Suggested donation: $6 US/$8 CDN/£4 UK
Order Code: **B2**
On Audiocassette: $9 US/$12 CDN/£6 UK
Order Code: **B2AC**

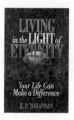

Living in the Light of Eternity
K.P. Yohannan lovingly yet candidly reminds Christians of their primary role while here on earth: harvesting souls. This book challenges us to impact on eternity.

Suggested donation: $8 US/$10 CDN/£4.50 UK
Order Code: **B4**
On Audiocassette: $9 US/$12 CDN/£6 UK
Order Code: **B4AC**

Reflecting His Image
You've read it, now share it with a friend or family member!

Suggested donation: $8 US/$10 CDN/£4.50 UK
Order Code: **B5**

Exciting Videos

Cry of the Unreached

K.P. Yohannan speaks straightforward from the pulpit of Dr. Charles Stanley's church in Atlanta. This message will challenge you, convict you and awaken you to the potential of living a life more in tune with God's heart.

Suggested donation: $6 US/$8 CDN/£8.50 UK
Order Code: V2

Glad Sacrifice

This exciting 23-minute video shows real-life native missionaries spreading the Gospel across Asia. As you watch these dramatic scenes you will want to rejoice in God's plan to reach Asia for Christ.

Suggested donation: $6 US/$8 CDN/£8.50 UK
Order Code: V3

Christ's Call: "Follow My Footsteps"

In this compelling 41-minute video, K.P. Yohannan challenges us to follow in Christ's footsteps—steps that will deliver us from our self-centeredness and cause us to impact the lost millions in our generation.

Suggested donation: $6 US/$8 CDN/£8.50 UK
Order Code: V1

Operation Boot Camp

This 15-minute video will transport you to India and take you inside one of Gospel for Asia's intensive training centers. Learn why the training is so challenging. Meet young men who are willing to lay down their lives to reach the unreached of Asia.

Suggested donation: $6 US/$8 CDN/£8.50 UK
Order Code: V4

Driven to the Extreme!

This exciting 15-minute video will put you in the driver's seat as a Gospel for Asia van team takes the Gospel where it has never gone. See how this effective tool helps native missionaries penetrate deep into unreached territory.

Suggested donation: $6 US/$8 CDN/£8.50 UK

Order Code: **V5**

Built on the Solid Rock

This 15-minute video documents how Gospel for Asia's church-planting ministry is exploding across previously unreached areas of the 10/40 Window. See lives being transformed for eternity as people turn to Christ.

Suggested donation: $6 US/$8 CDN/£8.50 UK

Order Code: **V6**

SEND!—Voice of Native Missions

Stay informed! Exciting bimonthly newsmagazine.

Suggested donation: FREE, postage paid

Order code: **S1**

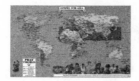

World Map

Allow God to burden your heart for the lost with GFA's 21.5x36 inches "Pray for the World" Map. Also available laminated.

Suggested donation: $5 US/$8 CDN

Order Code: **MAP**

Laminated Suggested donation: $8 US/$11 CDN/£5 UK

Order Code: **MAPL**

Please send the following materials:

Code	Quantity	Donation
B2	E X A 1 M P L E	$6.00

Postage Enclosed—US
1-4 items—$1 per item
5-10 items—75¢ per item
11+ items—10%   _____

Postage Enclosed—CDN
10%, $3 minimum   _____

Additional donation   _____

Total donation enclosed: _____

Name _____

Address _____

City _____

State/PRCounty _____ Zip/PC _____

Country _____ Phone (_____) _____

☐ **Please send me information on how to sponsor a native missionary.**

Mail Order to: Literature Department, Gospel for Asia, 1932 Walnut Plaza, Carrollton, TX 75006

Or phone 1-800-WIN-ASIA (946-2742), also visit our web site: www.gfa.org

In Canada: Gospel for Asia, 120 Lancing Dr. Unit 6, Hamilton ON L8W 3A1
Or phone 1-800-681-ASIA (681-2742)

In U.K.: Call 01323-645088 for ordering information

In Germany: Call 49-7623-5834 for ordering information

Make all checks payable to Gospel for Asia. Please allow four to six weeks for delivery.
All gifts to Gospel for Asia are tax deductible less the fair market value of the materials you receive from us. The suggested donations are at or below the fair market value of each item and are subject to change.

Date Due

B&H

Code 4386-04, CLS-4, Broadman Supplies, Nashville, Tenn., Printed in U.S.A.